ALSO BY HARRIET RUBIN

The Princessa: Machiavelli for Women

The World's Greatest Poem

and How It Made

History

Dante in Love

HARRIET RUBIN

SIMON & SCHUSTER

New York London Toronto Sydney

SIMON & SCHUSTER
Rockefeller Center
1230 Avenue of the Americas
New York, NY 10020

SIMON & SCHUSTER and colophon are registered trademarks of
Simon & Schuster, Inc.

Book design by Ellen R. Sasahara

For information regarding special discounts for bulk purchases,
please contact Simon & Schuster Special Sales at 1-800-456-6798 or
business@simonandschuster.com

Manufactured in the United States of America

10   9   8   7   6   5   4   3   2   1

Library of Congress Cataloging-in-Publication Data is available.

ISBN 0-7432-3446-4

For Steven Lowenstam (1945–2003)

di tante cose quant' i' ho vedute,
dal tuo podere e da la tua bontate
riconosco la grazia e la virtute.

through your power and your excellence alone
have I recognized the goodness and the grace
inherent in the things I have been shown.

(*Paradiso* 31.82–84; trans. Ciardi)

Contents

modestly human to the level of high art, defines the third element of achievement in these expansionist times. Throughout Italy, the search for the grail shifts to the search for sugar, cinnamon and gold. Dante experiences this double, squinting time of spiritual forces and commerce as he enters the wilderness of the Inferno.

4. The Ogre of the Brotherhood   *63*

The death of poet Guido Cavalcanti, Dante's first friend and "brother" in the Fedeli d' Amore—"the brotherhood of the faithful in love." Was Dante responsible? The birth of poetry; the first time the word "love" is uttered and Dante's vow to write what had never been written before. The blend of asceticism and passionate desire that led to conflicts among the brotherhood. Dante's sorrows take on a new depth as he travels deeper into the Inferno.

5. The Golden Sperm   *87*

How Dante constructed the Comedy. *The poet vies with the ghost of St. Thomas Aquinas, author of "that other epic," the* Summa Theologica, *to lift poetry from its bookish deadness. He studies "alchemy"—literally, "golden sperm"—for a new language, and finds a means by which loss can be reversed.*

6. The Difficult Discipline of "As Pleased Another"   *111*

Can failure be reversed? Wandering the open roads of Italy, an outcast and fugitive with a death warrant hanging over his head, Dante compares himself to the heroic wanderer Ulysses and his failed last voyage. To what can one aspire that is free of the deadlock of ambition? One can try to see morally and aesthetically, looking for the divine in things, learning to read "the mystery of history," which is that "God writes straight with crooked lines."

Part III: Purgatorio (1308-12)

7. Virgin Discoveries   *135*

A woman takes on the role of a god. Dante, in the midst of this revolution, discovers the feminine mysteries. Something very dramatic had happened between the two notions of tenderness: piety and pity—between ancient warrior Aeneas's pious devotion to his father and Michelangelo's Renaissance Pietà: the sculpture of a young woman cradling her dead son in her lap. Out of this, the definition of genius becomes linked with sweetness. Dante prepares for meeting his dead lover, Beatrice.

8. Number-Crunchers in Paris   *157*

The abduction of the papacy to Avignon, dashing hopes for a new Roman Empire. Dante voyages to Paris in 1309 in the wake of the pope. The new sciences and Gothic churches fill his imagination and provide him the means for Paradise and Paradiso: "sacred geometry," apparent in the magisterial Gothic cathedrals that are rare in Italy but which dominate France.

9. "We Have Tears for Things," Said Virgil   *183*

The saddest moment in literature is not when Juliet dies undeflowered, Byron said, but when Virgil leaves Dante at the pinnacle of Purgatory. The ghost of the great ancient poet has guided his protégé Dante through Hell, which he knows all too well, up the Mountain of Purgatory and then disappears when the student surpasses the teacher with his newfound certainty.

Part IV: Paradiso (1316-21)

10. What the Bread God Wished

*Inside the mind of God, fully and at last, Dante learns how to see
beyond human sight. Dante reaches this pinnacle in his fifties in
Ravenna, truly a secret Paradise. The High Middle Ages is ripening
to its death. The poet completes his greatest and most modern work,*
Paradiso, *as chaos threatens. Dante's death, and his restless bones.*

PART I

Touching the Depths

CHAPTER 1

A Time Run by Dreamers
and Their Dreams

ON JANUARY 27, 1302, A COURIER ON A DEADLY MISSION arrives in bone-chilling Rome off the wintry paths from Florence. He bears a message for Dante Alighieri. Alighieri, who is thirty-six, is not yet the great Dante, author of the poem that will become like a religion to artists and statesmen and other seekers of perfection. Alighieri is in Rome on a doomed diplomatic mission—a lethal pattern which seems to characterize the majority of his efforts. About most things Alighieri is cautious and indirect. Though he holds strong views, he seldom acts on them. He never told the woman he most loved of his feelings for her; and now that she is dead, words are meaningless. He expresses himself in precious verses that circulate among a small circle of his friends. He has tried everything, from law to war, and from politics to teaching, with mixed results. So why is this unthreatening father of three the object of a decree that is equivalent to a hanging— exile—and not even singling him out for a brave act, but accusing him of barratry or breach of duty along with 359 others—an undignified lottery. He has simply found himself on the wrong side of an old political skirmish. His death notice is inconsequential to an observer of 1302—it is a tree falling in the forest.

But the consequences will surprise the world: the edict will force Dante to take no other course than the pursuit of the education of his soul over the nearly two decades of brutal exile. The sentence will unsettle us more than seven hundred years later. Genius, happiness, love and vision will hereafter be measured by how Alighieri handles the awful sentence he receives this day. He will develop self-knowledge and self-mastery, brutal honesty combined with melting sweetness. Dante Alighieri represents the height and depth of a turning point in time. The years 1300–1320 are the pinnacle of the period known as the High Middle Ages, the foundation of modern commerce, art and faith. They are aptly named for the elation they inspire—when genius ruled over laws and sometimes coursed out of control.

The essential question is: How did Dante become Dante? Why didn't his fate silence him forever, reduce him to desiccating anguish? How did a man who had been unable to express his passion reinvent the nature of love and genius? How did he reverse his failures? How does one voice become the most important voice?

Dante in Love suggests a love story, and some might expect this to be the tale of sweethearts beyond the grave: Dante and Beatrice, legendary lovers, divided by death, reunite in a poetic afterlife. In fact, it is a truer love story: that of a dispossessed soul learning the meaning of life and finding the grace to love that meaning. Attaining that kind of love depends on developing "the good of the intellect," Dante wrote.

The Divine Comedy has exerted a shaping influence on the lives of a wide range of people: poets (T. S. Eliot, Ezra Pound and hundreds of others), writers (George Eliot, Primo Levi, Tom Stoppard), psychologists (Sigmund Freud and Carl Jung), philosophers

(David Hume, Georg Wilhelm Hegel), rock stars (Patti Smith and Bruce Springsteen), as well as butchers, bakers, air force pilots and political figures. One can ask without exaggeration: How did this poet help steer the medieval world into the modern one? In our time, we may wonder, what will the modern world coalesce into, and given that to a certain extent we can author our fortune and fate, can we look to visionaries, not merely soldiers and bureaucrats, to guide us?

What follows is a tale for those who have dreamed of creating something that seems beyond them. Its purpose is not to save you a lifetime of reading one book, *The Divine Comedy*, but to start you on the project.

★

AT THE BEGINNING, the roads that link Dante to his fate are the Jubilee roads which two years earlier Pope Boniface VIII had smoothed over, summoning all the world to Rome in one massive celebration for the eternal church. The poor and the lame, the rich and the mighty, had arrived by the thousands to fill Rome's streets and, better still, Boniface's coffers. All roads lead to Rome. In October 1301, Alighieri was sent there from Florence by his political party, the White Guelfs. He had been one of the party's priors in Florence for ten years, the equivalent of a junior senator. He was there to ask for Boniface's help in stopping the fighting and threats of civil war inside Florence, but the wily and ambitious pontiff set a trap for the delegation. He has bought time for his own armies to march into Florence and claim the city as his personal treasure. These were years when artistic genius seemed to stop for papal politics and all of Roman ingenuity got channeled into a grab for land and money. Florence was a prize, and Boniface wanted it. In truth, he wanted everything. Dante, drawn into the pope's web, will realize only much later that he was duped by his hopes and dreams into believing that appeals to reason might forge a peace.

As the priors were waiting to make their appeals, the pope was masterminding a change of guard in Florence to the opposition party of Black Guelfs, "guelf" being a term perhaps derived from the German word for "wolves." News of the handover of the city will reach Alighieri and his peers in the form of the decree of exile.

The decree condemns the faction of Guelfs known as Whites on charges of opposition to the pope and of having stirred up violence in Florence. It demands that Alighieri return home immediately to defend himself in a trial. Dante does not return to Florence, and on January 27, 1302, he is condemned to two years of exile, barred from holding public office and required to pay a ruinous fine of 5,000 florins within three days. On March 10, Dante's goods are ordered confiscated and he is condemned to death by burning if he should fall into Florentine hands. The Florentine fathers prefer ashes to corpses where their enemies are concerned. They are, after all, Romans at heart and as such are believers in ghosts. "Let the earth lie lightly on you" is how they say good night rather than goodbye to their freshly buried dead. As for the threat of seizure of the accused's scant remaining assets, Alighieri has already had trouble paying his bills. Confiscating his property will reduce his family—Gemma, his wife, and their two sons and daughter—to destitution.

The sentence against Alighieri does not seem extreme in Florence, where factionalism is just one manifestation of widespread disunity. The idea of a united Italy is unimagined in 1302. The

majority of Italians have never heard the word "Italy." It is a country in which only the intellectuals live, those who read the word
in the great books. Unity is a dream. Divisions exist in cities, on
streets and between neighbors; hatreds are acted upon. Justice is
impossible to find. Rioters run loose. The prisons have been
thrown open; nobles and criminals rob, kidnap and kill. Heiresses
are forced to marry impromptu suitors, and fathers compelled to
sign rich settlements.

Rome, the seat of emperors and popes who believed themselves masters of the world, is in the hands of the power-hungry.
When Albert of Austria named himself emperor on the death
of Adolphus of Nassau in 1298, Boniface, in his rage, placed the
crown on his own head, seized a sword and exclaimed, "It is I who
am Caesar, it is I who am emperor, it is I who will defend the rights
of the empire." In May 1347, Cola di Rienzi, a washerwoman's son
born in year eleven of Dante's nineteen-year exile, became tribune
of Rome. He pointed his sword to the sky and three-quarters of
the globe and declared, "This and this and that too is mine."

But Florence, eternal Rome's rising competitor, is the mad and
dreamy sister. Florence is gambling on the symbols of power—
banking, art, science—rather than on armies or imperial tyrannies
to rule Europe. For the next two hundred years, her dominance in
literature, architecture, finance and technology will be unquestioned. The sword will become powerless against the thought and
the florin.

Florence will become the most brilliant and the "most damned
of Italian cities," the poet Ezra Pound wrote in the early twentieth
century, complaining that "there is neither place to sit, stand or
walk." An editorial in *La Repubblica* in 2000, seven hundred years
after Boniface's Jubilee, complained that men were suffering heart

attacks in growing numbers from climbing too many stairs for midday trysts, their daily jubilees: Why weren't city planners requiring landlords to install elevators? Annoyance is the city's steady pulse. She is often nasty with her proudest sons, demanding their best work and then excommunicating them or, if they stay, hanging or incinerating them.

Galileo, after lecturing about Dante's *Commedia* in universities throughout Italy in the 1500s, will be condemned to torture and death for holding the theory that the sun, not the earth, is the center of the universe. Machiavelli will be dismissed from the Medici court, sent first to prison to be stretched out on the rack, and then thrust into penury for the rest of his life. Giordano Bruno, the Renaissance freethinker who scoffed at the mysteries of faith, will be chased to Rome, where he will be burned in public, in the Campo dei Fiori. Ambition, heresy, rage—these are virtues in the cultural temperament of Florence. The Renaissance's most dangerous ideas have precedent in Dante. But ideas alone do not sharpen Florence's edges. Three classes divide its secular life: the *popolo minuto,* or "little people"—shopkeepers and artisans; the *popolo grasso,* or "fat people"—wealthy employers or businessmen; and the *grandi,* or big shots—the nobles. Wars are always simmering and often erupting. "The only thing that's changed in several hundred years," said one twenty-first-century Italian, "is that Lorenzo de' Medici introduced lemon trees to Italy in the 1500s."

*

THE BRAWL BETWEEN the Guelfs and the Ghibellines of the 1300s is more than a bit *opera buffa,* and even by these standards, it reaches burlesque proportions. On Easter 1215, a young married woman had flirted in public with a man not her husband. He flirted back. A vendetta was declared between Guelf and Ghibel, two rival brothers of Pistoia related to the amorous couple, and dozens of recriminations later, the fighting spun out of control.

The ancient myth of Rome's founding by twin brothers Romulus and Remus, who were nursed by a she-wolf, marked a violent beginning of brotherly murder. In medieval Tuscany, two rival brothers grew into two distinctive brotherhoods: the Guelfs, though mighty and great, were born as vassals; the Ghibellines, as gifted intellectuals. Their differences were like those of modern gangs: the Ghibellines wore feathers on the left side of their caps, the Guelfs on the right. At table, Ghibellines cut fruit crosswise, Guelfs straight down. Ghibellines wore white roses, and Guelfs red. But while there was room in the Ghibelline state for giants who preserved the might and prowess of ancient heroes, never in the Guelf state would there be mental room for Ghibelline brains. The extremes met in the contest of "the Sword" between Otto IV and Sicilian Frederick II—intellectual, poet, philosopher—who would become emperor of Rome in July 1215 after defeating Otto in the Battle of Bouvines in 1214. Otto was known as a boor who managed to anger the princes with whom he came into contact, even when his edicts were wise and just. When he was dethroned, the priests forced his confession and then beat him to death with rods. Guelf and Ghibelline became synonymous with support for the pope on the one hand and the emperor on the other. The late thirteenth century was growing too intellectual for legitimate Guelf rule, so they went on the attack, supported by the pope.

The violence kept shifting, and so did the violent. The sides were least clearly marked among the brawlers. "This is the disease of Florence at work: parthenogenesis; the splitting of simple life forms," says Dante scholar John Freccero. Factions split into atoms: the Guelfs split into two opposite factions, and Dante became a Ghibelline-Guelf, or a "White," as opposed to a member of the "Black" faction. The feud sucked in every frustration, every long-simmering antagonism from politics to money to envy. Everything got expressed in the violence that followed and, thanks to the muddy ground of politics, never seemed to end.

Boccaccio said of Dante that he would have been unable to create his work if he had not been a Ghibelline, inspired by the legendary secular and intellectual light that bordered, often, on heresy. This was the price they paid: three hundred and fifty-nine White Guelfs, the intellectual aristocracy of which Dante numbered himself, were sentenced to death in 1302, but most were allowed to escape into exile. Fourteen hundred houses were destroyed, leaving the center of Florence in ashes.

*

ALIGHIERI IS NO HERO. He is no Aeneas chased by winds of destiny to found a new nation; he is no Paul who can organize resistance into a religion. He is to be pitied. He is gauche. He doesn't know how to behave, how to act, what to say. He often loses himself in books and ideas. If Dante thought he could survive on his wits alone outside of Florence as he had inside the city, he would have been the only one to place a bet. At the time of his exile, he is a second-rate poet, the author of some ballads and one book, *La Vita Nuova,* which few would remember had he not written the *Comedy.* The *Vita Nuova* is written in a sentimental style typical of its time. It reminds modern readers of the damp allegories of John Bunyan's Christian sweating his way through the Valley of Death. An indifferent provider for his family, a diplomat whose strong suit is not diplomacy and a love poet who never professed his love: now he adds fugitive to his résumé. Following the order of the decree, he leaves Rome, we don't know how or exactly when. But he takes cover in Siena, a mighty rival of Florence, in whose narrow and crooked streets he would be safe. There he plots with his fellow exiles how they might defy the pope and return to Florence. When they cannot agree on an approach, Alighieri splits off from the pack.

*

EXILE IS THE death of identity. This death is as real as actual death. Home, career, history: all that defines a man suddenly seems an illusion. Even his age of thirty-six years seems untethered by certainty. Some days on the open road, he must feel as unsure as a ten-year-old; other days as weak as an old man of a hundred.

Exile is the punishment reserved for the largest transgressions. Cities were walled to protect against madmen, beasts, enemies and even some of the ravages of weather. The world was a frightening place. The men and women of the time were much more exposed to nature than we are, and nature was much less tamed. Nights were darker; animals, prowling and fierce. Wolves from the mountains starve in the cold and birds stick to the trees in the frost. Wanderers are vulnerable to hailstorms, and a cloudless heaven can raise a plague of beetles from the cracked dry earth. The weather was already growing disastrously colder in 1300, and the growing seasons were becoming shorter—the first signs of economic trouble in Europe, though no one knew then of the catastrophe that loomed. The plague, forty years hence, will take a devastating toll on an already hungry population.

The exile straying from his native town in Italy in 1302 would lose his speech because there was no common language by which he could be understood. To move from one town to another less than thirty miles away called for sharp revision of attitudes and knowledge.

The roads Alighieri walked often gave way to overgrown paths, dense with briars, thick with trees hiding thieves. The paths led to swamps, where travelers would sicken and die in hours. A road might end at a rough bridge built by a hermit who lived on the charity of the passersby. Alighieri would have to have a coin for the crossing. Adept travelers would not leave home without a hen or two under their arm, or a flagon of homemade wine to use for tariffs. If the tolls were high, they would have to retrace their steps home and come back with a pig or calf.

For the next five of his nineteen years in exile, it will be as if Dante Alighieri, like the ancient Roman wanderer Ethico, had vanished into the bleak mountain fastness. The road he took from Rome was the road by which hordes of boys and girls in 1212, nearly ninety years earlier, had poured into Italy, seized with a blind and passionate fanaticism known as the Children's Crusade—ill-starred youngsters moving to their inevitable destruction. His epic life now begins. Dante—from this point he needs only one name—will live at large, "begging my life," as he said. "How many pairs of sandals did he wear out on the narrow goat paths of Italy?" the prisoner-poet Osip Mandelstam wondered from inside his Stalinist gulag, where his own shoes were confiscated.

Leaving the company of his fellow exiles in Siena, Dante walked northward alone, up the upper Arno valley past Sabbiano and Rassina, past La Verna, where St. Francis of Assisi received the stigmata, to Bibbiena, to the Passo dei Mandrioli down to Castrum Balnei (now Bagno di Romagna), place of healing waters, to Cesena at the edge of the wide Po plain, and then on to the sanctified hermitage of Camaldoli. He will eventually travel as far as France, Venice and perhaps even Oxford, England—scholar Paget Toynbee speculates. In Paris, Dante studied metaphysics at the University of Paris, where Abelard met his two great loves, ideas and Héloïse, and aspired to a third, the love of God. The exact whereabouts of a fugitive who effectively evaded the law in the fourteenth century are impossible to trace. But we know approximately where Dante traveled by what he records in the *Comedy* and by a few eyewitness reports published a generation after his death.

Those places will assume a mythic character to generations of travelers ever after. Dante's Verona is the Verona of Romeo and Juliet: in *Purgatorio 6*, he writes as if he knew the Montecchi (the Montagues) and Cappelletti (the Capulets). His Verona is a home in Hell for his old teacher, Brunetto Latini. Venice is even lower, in the boiling pits of the deceivers (*Inferno* 21.7–18). Six hundred years later, Thomas Mann's Aschenbach will find a room at the Lido and fall in love with a beautiful young boy, a Beatrice-like character, a figure of eternal youth, to whom he never speaks. Dante's voice echoes in these cities.

Sometimes Dante is welcomed by friends, but more often he heads to the center of the town, hangs his hat on a post and hopes some stranger will pick it up. The custom is that whoever takes a journeyer's hat promises him a night's free lodging, sometimes in a barn where he must lie beside students, merchants or illiterate vagabonds and also the cows. Peasants reported to Bruni, a fifteenth-century biographer, that Dante often spent days looking down at the river while writing, they assumed, a book on the nature of fish.

Food was another matter. Not until he was the guest of wealthy patrons sporadically over the first decade of exile did Dante slake his hunger with pasta, chopped liver or pigeon. More likely his stomach was only washed with water and bean or squash soup poured over dried bread. Fresh bread was expensive. Tomatoes, which modern travelers think of as quintessentially Italian, were not eaten until the sixteenth century, and the Tuscans were the first Europeans to take the risk because, cut open, the inner pulp had the appearance of the cross. Dante will rue the salty bread of strangers. His wants seemed to be fed by petty thievery of his hosts—not money, but a pen or a knife.

Biking through Tuscany or sipping limoncello under Tuscan or Umbrian skies today, one cannot imagine Dante's fate as Hell, which is what he calls it. The modern wayfarer shares perhaps only one quality with Dante: today one is not on the march but is alienated from oneself. Settled in one place, one commonly wants to be in another. We are restless. The philosopher George Santayana, imagining Dante's exile, wrote:

> What is life but a form of motion and a journey through a foreign world? Locomotion—the privilege of animals—is perhaps the key to intelligence. The roots of vegetables (which Aristostle says are their mouths) attach them fatally to the ground and they are condemned like leeks to suck up whatever suste-

nance may flow to them at the particular spot where they happen to be stuck.

In animals the power of locomotion changes all this pale experience into a life of passion; and it is on passion, although we anemic philosophers are apt to forget it, that intelligence is grasped.

Pope Gregory the Great, who lived from 540 until 604, said that the earth is like a hotel bed, a place to rest the body for a brief night. By "brief night," he meant a lifetime as measured by eternity. But he also meant that to make yourself a stranger to the world is to expect nothing but perfection. To wander constantly is to expect to find something more somewhere else: a paradise, maybe, or the secrets of life. Gregory believed one has to make oneself a stranger to the world, to refuse all the earth has to offer, to move upward and become a true citizen of heaven. The exile can easily feel he is a deposed king, someone special, a Lear looking to regain his rightful throne.

And yet, Dante's election to exile is also gratuitous, a gift from on high. Out of this tragedy, he can feel he is like a god, as solitary, vain and as despairing. Dante looks for cover of darkness, the source of light—the same as God. Both hide. Out of his loss, Dante discovers a kind of creative force he might never have known he possessed. He finds the path to his creative genius by placing the ego second to a larger talent or energy some call nature, some call the Muse and some call God. He doesn't arrive at "resolution." He masters poetry and what was considered in his time vision. Dante could have returned to Florence with the city's permission later in his exile. He chose to remain in exile. What was he seeking?

The rational world wasn't enough. What he discovered, like the great thirteenth-century philosopher Thomas Aquinas before him, was that absolutely rigorous argument can lead to mutually exclusive positions. Examining the light of stars, for example, as proof of God's existence, one eventually discovers that light behaves according to scientific principles, and God recedes from view. In 1300, Dante had experienced the death of his closest friend and mentor Guido Cavalcanti, a death he may have felt he caused by sending Cavalcanti into his own exile in one of his only acts of political power. Cavalcanti's death had followed soon after the death of the young woman Dante loved.

Dante decided reason meant nothing and he shifted to a different basis of knowledge. He remembered that there were certain things he couldn't say to Beatrice while she was alive. He felt that to say them would sound petty or untrue. Knowledge and faith—on which he had relied—couldn't capture what he felt. How could he express his love for her—or his guilt over Guido—without lapsing into cliché?

Every schoolchild knows that Beatrice is the goddess in Dante's imagination. But who was she? If Dante never spoke a word to her and she merely greeted him in *La Vita Nuova,* we ought to wonder why this love drove him and sustained him. Was she desirable because she was unattainable? But Dante "attained" her—loving her more deeply than most lovers can claim. He falls for her when she is a girl of nine and he a boy of ten. "Dark eros" even the most forgiving reader must charge him with. But he is nothing if not delicate, so much so that he never approaches her. Only their eyes meet. During the High Middle Ages, lovers cared more about contemplating their beloved object than about experiencing the feelings and sensations of the union. *"Che fa tremar di chiar-*

itate l'are," writes Cavalcanti—she "who makes the air all tremulous with light." One expected to find God in the eyes of one's beloved.

Beatrice Portinari was a well-to-do young woman whom Dante saw first as she was leaving a church, Florence's now famous La Badia, whose services overflow with seekers of the Dante–Beatrice magic. Beatrice's father was the Tuscan ambassador to France. At eighteen, she married Simone di Bardi, a son of the Bardi clan, one of the mighty banking families that loaned vast sums to kings and popes and brought the insurance industry to Italy when they began accepting risks on shipments of cloth. The family built the Bardi Chapel in Florence and commissioned Giotto to paint frescoes of the life of St. Francis in it. Dante will consign another of the Florentine bankers, Enrico Scrovegni, to that seventh circle of hell, suggesting his double dismay over Beatrice's marriage and her mate.

After Beatrice married, Dante married Gemma Donati; their contract was drawn in 1277, and the actual marriage took place in 1285. The names are clues to their characters: Gemma—gems, earthly artistry which all desire for their beauty and value. But Beatrice is blessedness, grace, that which resists time's transformations. For many years, scholars assumed Dante meant beatrice with a small *b*, until evidence was found establishing her as a historical figure.

Beatrice died at twenty-three in 1290 and Dante never stopped grieving for her. His exile will gain meaning when he realizes he can master loss and see her again. Memory holds the dead in our minds, but Dante discovers how to unseal these images so that the dead live for him. Having been stuck in a *dolce stil nuovo* habit of thinking—love as sweetness and suffering, the philosophy of the troubadour poets which he imbibed—he converted his exile into a search for new depths in language and experience. Poets say love and words can reverse failure and loss; Dante discovered how. His method is revealed to those who walk his hells and purgatories and find paradise. It is why Dante, though considered a Catholic poet, has as his greatest converts artists who have reached the end of technique and are eager to discover a new depth in the soul. Art without artifice: the *Commedia* makes the human being the text or canvas or song, and shows how one can oneself be revised. The artist, not the art, is revised.

★

THE PERIOD WE shall be observing most closely—as far back as 1290 and forward to 1321—is on the cusp of the High Middle Ages. These are the last years of youthful intoxication that young men experienced walking from Africa to Laon to Bologna searching for instruction into the meaning of life and apprenticing themselves to debaters in monasteries and cathedral schools, where the arts of memorization, meditation, sacred geometry, alchemy and faith drew forth stupendous art and discoveries. That had begun a hundred years earlier. Dante represents the beginning of a shift in the history of creativity: his is a time somewhat distanced from experience, exuberant still, but largely unfolding in the immortal space of the imagination, of allegory or symbolic meaning. With his peers, the products of the imagination take on the gravitas of age and experience. These three decades represent the height of the imagination, the creative life sandwiched between the Middle Ages and the Black Death.

The Middle Ages, roughly the period from A.D. 476 to 1492, have been described as a thousand years without a bath. The world was dark, the wars constant. By 1100, the population was booming and so were commerce, art and technology. The next two hundred years would be what historians call the High Middle Ages. The English Catholic writer G. K. Chesterton referred to them as "the Naissance, of which the Renaissance was a mere Relapse by comparison." Then a new century was born in 1300. Individualism flourished in such forms as paintings, literature, commerce, wealth and medicine. The culture reached a height and unity of purpose that some believe has never been repeated. From 1320 on, the economy stopped growing; bankruptcies increased; people starved. By the middle of the century, the Plague will have destroyed two-thirds of all Italy: 70 percent of the population of Venice and Genoa, for example. But until then, the spiritual and the physical are joined in an explosion of creativity. Gone are the legions of quibblers locked in relentless dispute. By the early 1300s, art and technology, banking and nation-building, individualism and faith, joined with results that still resonate. The modern world is born in the High Middle Ages, and it is not that medievals were modern, but that we think medievally.

"The Indian Summer of civilization," as Princeton University art historian Richard Krautheimer called it, was a time governed by dreamers and dreams. "Indian Summer" suggests a period when every color is present: a last deep gasp that cannot endure. Nature doesn't favor pinnacles, and there were seeds of destruction. The High Middle Ages are the root of all our contemporary "hot" problems, and "it is not surprising," says the Italian writer Umberto Eco, that "we go back to that period every time we ask about our origins." There was conflict between church and state. Trade unions were formed; the technological transformation of labor made new demands on a tradition-bound populace. Major conflicts such as the Crusades ceased, but negotiation—"war waged with kisses"—took its place. Feudal life was not over.

Still, in the spectacular three decades, poets are the visionaries. The hunger is not yet largely for gold and glitter, but the desire to know the secrets of the world. It is not the darkness of ignorance that holds people, but that of the imagination commanding reality. People's minds are "almost constantly attentive to all manner of signs, dreams or hallucinations. No psychoanalyst has ever examined dreams more earnestly than the monks of the 11th or 12th century," according to historian Marc Bloch. There is almost no line between hallucination and sight. By 1300, the difference was beginning to assert itself. The clash between thought and action, love and spirit, called for a new unity.

Dante made himself the messenger of these enormous changes, absorbing them, articulating them in a new literary language—Italian—that the masses of his time who didn't know Latin could understand. He wanted to create a new language made of noble or courtly speech that might unify people beyond the limits of the thirty-six local dialects, according to Dante's count, which bred misunderstanding and factionalism as well as hideous sounds—his own Tuscan dialect he condemns as "obtuse and degraded." The period hoists him to tremendous heights of creativity, and he maps his climb in the *Comedy*. As Genesis, the first book of the Bible, is about the birth of the race, the *Divine Comedy* is about the genesis of the individual with the force of a whole race and its history behind him.

Which Dante are we talking about: the man, or the fugitive-pilgrim in a work called the *Divine Comedy*? Mostly we will consider Dante's two voices the same, asserting that the exile could say true things only under the safe guise of a story.

★

WHEN DANTE DIED in 1321, the city fathers of Florence tried to bring his now valuable bones back home. As the famous author of the *Inferno,* the most-talked-about canticle, Dante had refused to return to Florence, which he was invited to do in 1315. Later several attempts were made to steal back his corpse from his grave in Ravenna, where he finally settled, and rebury it in his native city. The thieves were foiled each time.

But back in 1302, he could go to Hell on his own, and so he did. *Inferno, Purgatorio* and *Paradiso:* these are the three canticles or episodes that comprise the *Commedia.* More than 14,000 lines—or "facets," said Mandelstam, imaging an "exact" and monstrous crystal—make up this poem that tracks the education of a soul: Dante's and ours. He transformed himself from pilgrim or searcher, lost in his own subjectivity and questions, into the universal poet, certain and transcendent. By finding his way through Hell, sometimes called the traps of the ego, Dante graduates to Purgatory to learn the art of loss. From there, he undergoes many tests until he is admitted into the mind of God, from whose perspective he can see the meaning of sorrow and joy and everything in between.

Charles Dickens will offer his own story of life's comedy in *A Christmas Carol.* In his version of the Inferno, "Christmas Past,"

Ebenezer Scrooge confronts his miserly ways. In "Christmas Present," or Purgatory, he repairs his past; and in "Christmas Future," Paradise, he delights in the pleasure of a revised and newly well spent life. Dante had been a Scrooge with his own life and talent—until that cold day in Rome when his future finally caught up with him.

CHAPTER 2

The Difference Between One Who Knows and One Who Undergoes

THERE ARE TWO QUESTIONS BEFORE US. THE FIRST IS:
How did Dante become Dante? The second is: How can a reader
of this poem become, like Dante, a great crafter too, whom life's
losses do not undermine, but inspire?

Generations of readers have considered the *Comedy* a grail, an
energy secret, which they use as a lesson plan in creativity and
genius. These are people who depend on stories to show them
the way. They become apprentices of Dante, of *"il miglior fabbro,"*
the best artist, to meet the creative challenges of life. This is how
Thomas Stearns Eliot became T. S. Eliot following Dante's influence; or how doctors reading Dante become poet-physicians, or
builders become master craftsmen or politicians become visionary statesmen, by following the "reborn" poet who taught himself
to read the deepest meaning of life that wakes him from the sleep
of deadened habit. To solve this mystery requires that we learn
how the experiences along Dante's track trigger mirrorlike (or
"mimetic") changes in oneself. How do Dante's best students read
Dante?

★

SOME SAY IT takes two lifetimes to learn, as Dante did, how to make words burn, bleed and transport one to a pinnacle of god-like insight—prized lessons for those in positions of leadership or persuasion. Dante lived two lives, his ordinary life of thirty-seven years, and then his creative life of over seven hundred years, beginning with his exile in 1302. Dantisti believe they also have the chance to live two lives in one. Otherwise one might be tempted to cry out like the poet Calderón on his deathbed, "Dante, why were you so difficult?"

Embarking on this journey through the text as Dante embarked on it in his life, one must give up the safe distance that says of the *Comedy* that "It's only a story." Nietzsche wrote, "Dante is a hyena making verses among the tombs," remarking the work's unusual power to get under the reader's skin. Nietzsche, an unflappable student of power, had a mixture of respect for and fear of the poet who parted the curtains on what happens between the grave and the cradle. People submit to the hyena's voice to experience the power of the "passive intellect"—the imagination—and to see the hidden things that facilitate the search for meaning. Reading Dante is more like submitting to an undertow than like being entertained or informed. One finds oneself living the work, meeting his characters in the people one knows, and circling in his fiendish circles, climbing his purgatorial terraces, and then, if one is lucky, seeing light, not just seeing through it, an experience he calls Paradise. As one reads the *Comedy,* one is not at, but beyond, the boundaries of knowledge.

The book that reads *you,* is how the *Comedy* has been described. Dante set down a detailed and beautiful map of the mental universe he traveled. A work that is both art and a description of the making of its maker is unique. Who can follow the brush strokes into the heart of a black Rothko canvas and say for sure how one layer of midnight blue on a dark green surface led Mark Rothko, then a second-rate Picasso imitator, to discover Rothko, the singular voice? Looking at a Rothko canvas, we cannot follow the artist's decision points and passages to genius.

But Dante shows us the points of decision in his own life. Those followers who read the poem with an apprentice's eye say that the poet was not born a genius but taught himself the art of perfection. As he passes through the realms of unhappy and hopeful souls to find the key to bliss and perfection, he shows us that we are faced with the same decisions to rectify mistakes and think beyond the purely rational. We are invited, as he did, to talk to the dead and learn the secrets of happiness they wish they had known while alive. Those who cannot believe such knowledge exists have turned the poem into a puzzle, a work to be mined by scholars. So assiduous have the scholars been that a dean of Dante studies, John Hollander, suggests there may be more multivolume commentaries explaining the *Comedy* than there are on the Bible.

But there is another way to read Dante. Dante translated the sweep of social fortune—vast economic growth and radical institutional change—into a method of individual action. While borders between self and city, God and humanity, wealth and poverty, were being reshaped, Dante found an opening that permitted him to rethink human powers. One made one's own luck: that was the short of it. There is nothing else like this in literature: a work of genius that explains how it was created.

As Virgil, the great Roman poet, was Dante's guide, Dante shall be ours—with one caution: our Dante is not the professors' poet but the Dante who has been the creative, transformative force in countless lives over hundreds of generations: the Dantisti's *Comedy*.

★

EUROPEAN EDUCATION IN the early 1300s was an attempt to challenge the Platonic notion that it was necessary to banish poets from society. They are illusionists, Plato had warned, traffickers in emotion that undermine rational thought. The irony is that Plato's own writings are deeply poetic and Plato himself wrote poetry. He knew too well how the poet in him could take command of the thinker. Florence in the High Middle Ages worshiped Virgil as a prophet who had predicted the coming of Christ (in 40 B.C.!) More often than not, poets become leaders—and leaders become poets: Mohandas Gandhi, Martin Luther King, Vaclav Havel, "Il Magnifico" Lorenzo de' Medici, Marcus Aurelius, and Hadrian. They are forceful, perhaps, because politics for them come second to dreams, and perhaps even second to aesthetics. "Beauty is a weapon of mass destruction," said Joseph Connors, director of Florence's I Tatti, Bernard Berenson's foundation for Renaissance arts. He meant that encounters with beauty unsettle a person. Beauty is an imperative and a standard. It wipes away any excuse one has to be content with the ordinary. Beauty can and does change the world indelibly.

Many, including the poet Percy Shelley, have insisted that Dante is a social scientist "disguised" as a poet, and that his agenda is to create a society of creators. As Machiavelli studied princes to codify their deeds and shape subsequent generations into strong-armed princes, Dante studies poets to determine the education of the best crafters. Isaac Babel, the twentieth-century Russian writer, put it well: "The fondest children are the ones we make with our own hands. All masterful creations"—whether bridges, nations, policy or technical inventions—"exude poetry." A life force is in their work. "Each and every one of them contains a thought, a drop of eternity." To add a measure of immortality to that which one creates, it is necessary to study Dante's methods of creation.

Those who shudder at the thought of the humiliated god who tried to make a mighty bull and created a lumbering buffalo instead will understand. The ability to will one thing into being is the great challenge of life. Dante's formula is to exert determination, loyalty and faith in this endeavor. He knew that as there can be moral sin, so also there can be aesthetic sin. Thomas Aquinas wrote, "He who prefers what he most likes to what is most beautiful is said to 'miss the mark.' "

The idea of the model creator as God is intentional. As Dante says, he who would portray a figure cannot do so unless he becomes it, or as we might say, unless he *lives* it. This means that he—and we—must conform our intellect to the artist's so as to think with his mind and see with his eyes. Acts of self-renunciation are required of all those who aspire to live fully and fruitfully.

*

SUCH AMBITIONS HAVE their dangers. Some people lose themselves in Dante; they hear the hyena's voice. Mary Ann Evans, who wrote brilliant novels under the name George Eliot, married a young admirer at age fifty-three. They honeymooned in

Italy, where they studied Dante together. Reading of the love of a couple in Canto 5 of *Inferno*, the new bride turned to her young husband, John Cross, and declared that she expected their marriage would be a physical union, not just a spiritual one. Upon hearing this, Cross jumped from their balcony. He lived, and the marriage continued—happily, it is said.

The laughing hyena also got to his nineteenth-century scholar Gabriele Rosetti, an Oxford professor of Italian literature, who would name his son Dante. Rosetti wrote a feverish treatise about Dante's *Comedy* as a secret manifesto addressed to an elite Masonic society (that did not yet exist). His wife, fearing the assault to her husband's reputation that such a tract would arouse, begged friends to buy up all the copies in London bookshops so that she could burn them on the family's front lawn. Dantisti occasionally do not survive their descent into Hell or the climb into Purgatory.

But many followers fare better than Evans or Rosetti. Studying the *Comedy* to rescue himself from a bad marriage and creative uncertainty helped turn Tom Eliot into the great Eliot who wrote in homage to Dante and considered himself a modern-day Dante. Sigmund Freud read Dante in a creative crisis; scholar Henry Abelove of Wesleyan University says Freud's masterpiece, *The Interpretation of Dreams*, was not just inspired by *Inferno*, but was guided by it. The dreams in Freud's work have their parallel in the episodes of *Inferno*, and Freud backdated the work's publication to 1900 just as Dante backdated the publication and storyline of *Inferno* to 1300 from its release in 1308 or thereabouts. Some historians say that Dante released *Inferno* and *Purgatorio* together or within a year of each other, both by 1315. *Paradiso* was copied and circulated soon after Dante's death in 1321. Manuscripts were copied and distributed widely, and Dante's earliest admirers included the major late-fourteenth-century writers Boccaccio, Petrarch and Chaucer.

Galileo wrote and presented three lectures on mapping Hell as he was mapping the stars. Ross King, the author of *Brunelleschi's Dome,* describes Brunelleschi finding the measurements for building Florence's Duomo—regarded as an impossible task—through his study of Dante's architecture in *Inferno* and *Paradiso.* And Freya Stark, twentieth-century British writer in the then untraveled Middle East, brought only three things with her as she plunged alone into the Arab world: a revolver, a fur coat, and—as her map—a copy of *Inferno.*

*

BEFORE RESUMING THE story of how Dante became Dante, it is important to look at how his followers have read actively, not for information but for transformation. They say there is a difference between one who knows and one who undergoes. They consider the *Comedy* the fulfillment of Dante's promise "to remove those living in this life from a state of misery, and to guide them to a state of happiness." Happiness in mortal terms is a form of perfection.

Though Dante originally called his work *Vision,* he ended up referring to it as the *Comedy* because, unlike in tragedy, people are happy at the end. (The word *Divine* was added by others later.) To reach the state of lasting happiness meant finding the formula that reversed the lifelong losses of age, of love and of adaptation to circumstances. Freud or Jung may tell you what you've lost or misinterpreted, but Dante shows how to turn loss into salvation.

By current self-help standards, it is unusual for high art like the *Comedy* to be utilized to heal a reader, but not in the Middle Ages, when texts were not simply transmitters of information. They were not surfaces but depths one entered. Books were concavities. One disappeared into words.

It is best to read Dante as a child reads, Jorge Luis Borges has said—not to puzzle infinitely over meanings, but to imagine oneself inside the story of the work and the work's creation. A child reading *Harry Potter* may become Harry Potter. Apprentices of Dante read to become Dante. The rhythm of the poetry sets the reader a walking pace. *Terza rima* is a rhythm Dante invented, a gait: left, right, left; one step back for every two forward: ABA/BCB/CDC, and so on. It is a spiral, like the pilgrim's journey. "We are always going backwards to go forwards, attempting to find the new in the old," writes Professor Teolinda Barolini. The reader picks up the rhythm of Dante leaving behind the familiar for the new and unfamiliar, which can be a circle of discovery, doubt, and discovery:

> Nel mezzo del cammin di nostra vita
> mi ritrovai per una selva oscura,
> ché la diritta via era smarrita.

> Ahi quanto a dir qual era è cosa dura
> esta selva selvaggia e aspra e forte,
> che nel pensier rinova la paura!

> Tant'è amara, che poco è più morte
> ma per trattar del ben chi'i' vi trovai,
> dirò de l'atre cose, chi'i' v'ho scorte.

Halfway through the story of my life
    I came to in a gloomy wood, because
    I'd wandered off the path, away from the light.

It's hard to put words to what that wood was;
    I shudder even now to think of it,
    so wild and rough and tortured were its ways;

And death might well be its confederate
    in bitterness; yet all the good I owe
    to it, and what else I saw there, I'll relate.

              (*Inferno* 1.1–9; trans. Ciaran Carson)

Medieval thinkers had a common goal when lost in the woods of confusion or uncertainty, and that was to remember that they had the makings of a god in themselves. Jesus had been human. If a god had been made a man, why couldn't a man become a god? Their suffering is similar; perhaps so is their capacity for genius.

To find the godlike in themselves, those thinkers, including Dante, turned to every form of knowledge available, including alchemy. Some alchemists were spurred on by a greedy desire to manufacture gold from feathers or lead, but most were looking for a means of rising from the worldly, unstable, corruptible matter to a more perfect substance. Alchemy began as an Arab science eventually practiced by western scientists such as Roger Bacon and Isaac Newton. They asked: How can an idea, typically so powerful while in the mind, maintain its force when realized on paper, or in stone, or in words? Can a voice plunge through the confusion, the Babel Tower of multiple languages? Can the imperfectibility of man's creations aspire to a brilliance beyond even gold?

Medievals, it is said, often reduced the beautiful to the moral or useful. Dante gave moral values an aesthetic foundation. What do we have to be proud of except a striving for perfection in the things we do? Moderns make the idea of perfection harder to accomplish than it is. We have the wrong idea of perfection—we think that it requires flawlessness. In fact, it does not exclude imperfection. It only craves attention. Look and attend. And here love and beauty join: "The love of a thing," said the Dantisto Baruch Spinoza, "consists in the understanding of its perfections." The one, the true and the beautiful, said Aristotle and his disciple Aquinas.

The alchemists' ultimate question was: How can the perfect (i.e., God) create something imperfect (i.e., man)? Dante reads this message as: How can one become as God in creating one's own work? The *Comedy* offers us the best human tutorial on this subject.

The secret lay in the use of words and numbers. It was an old Roman ideal to own people's hearts and minds, not just dictate their behavior. "I want people to see my soul over my body," the Emperor Augustus wrote. To express true beliefs in deathless rhetoric was considered the height of power. Were words eternal, or was there some coded language inside them that expressed power?

Part of Dante's experience on the open road was to feel that he was unlocking esoteric secrets, exploring transmutation, as had the alchemists. A new understanding of change was occurring at the end of the 1200s: an interest in "radical change," writes historian Carolyn Bynum, "where an entity is replaced by something completely different. Even theologians were asserting that growth occurs because food changes into blood and bile—nutrition—and not because of a mysterious expansion of angelic light." Throughout Europe, as feudalism was crumbling, people found it increasingly possible to change their social roles: their jobs, their incomes, the class into which they could marry. Economic opportunities in the towns gave men new careers beyond that of a knight or a monk. Women could find an alternative to marriage by entering a monastery. But such freedom provokes fear and the need for limits. Establishing what is possible forces the development of individuality, and a sense of individuality is the fulcrum of change.

Change is the modern alchemist's stone. T. S. Eliot said people stay in Hell only because they cannot change. Can we trust that Dante changed? How real are the changes he underwent? Did he enter Hell or just imagine he did? Charles Singleton, who taught the undergraduate Eliot the *Comedy* at Harvard, maintained that Dante is telling a fiction whose ultimate fiction is that it is not a fiction. He meant that Dante indeed saw the hidden workings of the universe, even if he had to adopt fictional images such as devils and flying dragons to portray it. Dante says the soul can spend a human life span like a baby satisfied with the very simple and learn only when the truth is "sugared." Or it can advance. To do so, Dante will start it off with the brutal harum-scarum images of Hell, then the education in the arts that is the style of Purgatory, and finally the visions and revelations of Paradise.

So is Dante's story real or a fable? People weren't prone to make these distinctions in Dante's time. Giovanni Boccaccio, writing about Dante in the mid 1300s, talked to at least four people who claim to have known Dante in the flesh. He remarked that when the poet was in Verona and the fame of his work had spread, probably after 1308, he was known by sight to many, and his travels were unquestioned. "As he passed a group of women, one of them said to the others, 'Isn't that the man who goes down to Hell as he likes, and returns, and brings back news of them below?' To which the others replied, 'Indeed it must be him—do you not see how his beard is singed and his skin darkened by the heat and smoke that are below.'"

At the very end of the *Comedy,* Dante realizes that the love of God informs the universe down to the lowest pits of Hell. The artist sees the beauty everywhere and simply borrows it. "A little taste of ambrosia drips down into the lowest depths of hell," wrote the philosopher Joseph Campbell. To taste that perfection is to redeem oneself, feel for a moment free of the shadow falling between the idea—or word—and the thing itself. It is the point at which a reader has her best shot at becoming Dante, even momentarily.

Osip Mandelstam believed that Dante represented the point at which literary criticism becomes "living medicine." Dante, he says as he languished in Stalin's gulag, showed him how to be a "Houdini from Hell." Mandelstam, like others, learned how to incarnate his soul in the objects of his passions. There are ways to express ourselves so that our words become reality. *"Si che dal fatto il dir non sia diverso"*—"So that speech is not different from fact" (*Inferno* 32.12). Dante wants us to know that to tell the truth is not art or sport. Words are life. Words can be made flesh, not only in a religious sense, but in a secular sense.

Through words and numbers, those who follow Dante pursue perfection. Something perfect leaves nothing out. A small masterpiece by Picasso, for example *Woman with a Book,* has it all: every color and shape, the old and the new. An artist does not become perfect himself; rather he learns to surrender to a perfection already in the nature of order. When Beatrice descends into Hell to ask the great Virgil to guide Dante in his ascent, she says, "Love moved me and makes me speak."

There is another theme to watch for: the poet-visionary created his work not in the bloom of youth, but in the middle of his life, at a time of terrible crisis that we all experience. The body is beginning to fade, and a whole new constellation is breaking into one's life. Dante says he was lost in a dangerous wood. He was threatened there by three animals, symbolizing pride, desire and fear. Virgil, the personification of poetic insight, appears and conducts him through the labyrinth of Hell, which is the place of those who are chained to their avarice and fears—the false loves that distract them from their true talent and thereby deprive them of joy. Dante freed himself of depleting passions between the ages of thirty-six and fifty-six. How was this possible at a time of life when a taste for experimentation and vigor is less likely?

*

AFTER DANTE, LITERATURE does not again make any large-scale serious attempts to enter these regions of consciousness. It takes knowledge of what we've lost to try to regain it. Two centuries intervene between the dreams of Dante and those of Shakespeare. What was lost in the intervening years and never regained?

People read Shakespeare with no expectation that they will become Shakespeare. The very idea of reading Shakespeare to become him seems ridiculous. Shakespearians admire the aesthetic distance, writes Harold Bloom. When they read about Prince Hal, they do not see their own faces on the battlefield. But they are trembling with Dante among the bodies whirling in Hell. In his words, "Who paints a figure, if he cannot be it, cannot draw it"—*"Che pinge figura, se non può esser lei, no la può porre."* Shakespeare and other great artists delight, but Dante plunges us into a medieval psychology and its potent mix of creative pursuit.

T. S. Eliot read the *Comedy* all his life, saving Paradise for his sixties, when he hoped he would have the maturity to follow Dante to his limits. He loved Shakespeare differently: "Dante and Shakespeare divide the modern world between them," he said, "there is no third." Novelist and Dante scholar Matthew Pearl writes in response, "Dante's half of the world enlarges every year." Eliot remarks that one canto of the *Comedy* corresponds to a whole play of Shakespeare's, and the *Divine Comedy* as a whole to all of Shakespeare's work. "Shakespeare gives the greatest *width* of human passion; Dante the greatest altitude and greatest depth."

Ezra Pound says, "It is part of Dante's aristocracy that he conceded nothing to the world, or to opinion—like Farinata [the majestic Ghibelline general whose bearing seems to diminish Hell itself] he met his reverses 'as if he held Hell in great disdain.' Shakespeare, by contrast, concedes, succeeds and repents in one swift, bitter line: 'I have made myself a motley to the view.' "

We read Shakespeare. Or Proust. Or Homer. We exult in their stories. Dante reads us. He sees not just into his characters' souls, but into ours. "There are works of art which are beautiful objects and works of art which are keys or passwords admitting one to a deeper knowledge, to a finer perception of beauty; Dante's work is of the second sort," Pound insisted. He believed Dante's word had magic. Pound's last word in his *Pisan Cantos,* written from a barred cell in the criminal hold of St. Elizabeth's Hospital for the insane, is *aiuto,* the word for "help" in Dante's language.

From medieval Italy we have inherited nation-states, modern armies, modern languages, merchant cities, the struggle between the rich and the poor, the concept of heresy or deviation, "our notion of love as a devastating unhappy happiness," writes Umberto Eco.

We moderns are on Dante's track, whether we know it or not. We should know it. ". . . knowledge is ultimately self-knowledge—and self-knowledge," as the master of words Cicero writes, "is the soul seen by itself." To know ourselves is to plunge into the mysterious workings of the universe, God's mind, the devil's and our own.

PART II

Inferno *(1304-8)*

Inferno

Nel mezzo del cammin di nostra vita
mi ritrovai per una selva oscura,
ché la diritta via era smarrita.

Ahi quanto a dir qual era è cosa dura
esta selva selvaggia e aspra e forte
che nel pensier rinova la paura!

In the middle of the journey of our life, I came
to myself in a dark wood where the straight
way was lost.

Ah! how hard a thing it is to tell what a wild,
and rough, and stubborn wood this was, which
in my thought renews the fear.

(*Inferno* 1.1–6; trans. Wicksteed)

CHAPTER 3

The Fearful Infant Whose Ravenous Hunger Cannot Be Satisfied

... *rispuose, poi che lagrimar mi vide,*
"se vuo' camper d'esto loco selvaggio;

   ché questa bestia, per la qual tu gride,
non lascia altrui passer per la sua via,
ma tanto lo 'mpedisce che l'uccide;

   e ha natura sì malvagia e ria,
che mai non empie la bramosa voglia
e dopo 'l pasto ha più fame che pria. . . ."

And he replied, seeing my soul in tears:
   "He must go by another way who would escape
   this wilderness, for that mad beast that fleers*

before you there, suffers no man to pass.
   She tracks down all, kills all, and knows no glut,
   But, feeding, she grows hungrier than she was. . . ."
             (*Inferno* 1.92–100; trans. Ciardi)

---

* John Ciardi's translation is the closest to a rhymed *Comedy* that captures the majesty of Dante's meaning. The word "fleer," a rarefied usage, originated in the Middle Ages and means "to smirk or sneer in contempt or derision."

INFERNO'S FIRST TWO CANTOS MAY HAVE BEEN WRITTEN two or three years before Dante's exile, when Dante was still in Florence among his friends and family, working in politics. The evidence for the early dating of the poem is the poet's melancholy tone and amateurish style. Dante is not yet in a cold, vindictive rage, or even a stance of Dostoyevskian empathy with his enemies. The walls in his mind must have come crashing down at a time when life appeared most normal, and what Aligheri inferred lay in wait he may have desired as a necessary if terrible release. Why would he have written of his Hell years before the exile, except that the mystery and ecstasy of imagination were already calling him?

In January 1302, Dante is on the road between Rome and Siena, where he will spend his early fugitive months. On the first night of exile—only death is more bitter, he tells us—he came to grips with his aborted ambition. He "comes to" in the middle of "our" life, he writes, and his attention is drawn to three fierce animals that block his way. He feels world-weary, caught in stale words, stale ways of thinking and feeling. He sees in their terrible aspects the mistakes, the regrets of wasted lives, including his own. These animals block his way. Unlike traditional heroes, he doesn't grab his sword and fight them; he thinks about them. The reader wonders who or what they are. Already the human surface is melting away from its deeper reality: man is a wolf, lion and leopard to man. The animal instincts cover the soul, and it is into the kingdom of souls—the Inferno—that Dante is headed, to penetrate the secrets of life that only the condemned know. If he can understand the animal in man, he will get the knowledge he has sacrificed his life and comforts to discover.

. . . che paura non mi desse
la vista, che m'apparve d'un leone.

Questi parea, che contra me venisse
con la test' alta e con rabbiosa fame . . .

. . . I shook with dread
at the sight of a great Lion that broke upon me
raging with hunger, its enormous head

held high as if to strike a mortal terror
into the very air.

(1.44–47; trans. Ciardi)

The fiercest is the lion—the symbol and lure of power. At the turn of the century into 1300, that figure was the pope.

The largeness of Boniface VIII's schemes could not fail to attract Dante's attention and fascinate him. He seemed a figure worthy of the epithets attached to him: "Pilot of Peter's Ship," "Chief Shepherd," "Father of Fathers," "Gate Keeper of Heaven," but he came to be known as "the warrior pope" and would be remembered as lacking all mercy and justice. "He came in like a fox, he ruled like a lion, he died like a dog," his epitaph reads.

Boniface had been trained in the strict intellectual discipline of the University of Paris. He was an intellectual and lover of the arts. He brought to Rome Giotto, Dante's friend. Boniface founded the University of Rome and vastly extended the Vatican Library. He was an astute and brilliant canonist and was spoken of in Dante's day as Dante himself would be talked about a generation later. Not until Michelangelo confronted Medici popes Leo X and Clement VII would another religious figure so confound an artist's life.

When Boniface was elected pope on January 23, 1294, he was over seventy and vain. The papacy was the strongest and the richest government in Europe. His investiture was met with enormous ill will for he had convinced his predecessor, the saintly but incompetent Celestine V, to resign after a mere five months. He ordered Celestine, then eighty, kept in detention in Rome, but he escaped, was captured and escaped again. Like a mouse under the gaze of a teasing cat, Celestine wandered for weeks through Apulia, reached the Adriatic, attempted a crossing, was wrecked, and then was cast ashore in Italy only to be brought back before Boniface, who condemned him to imprisonment in a narrow cell at Ferentino. Ten months later, he died.

Boniface tried to stir up sympathy for a new crusade, but the cities resisted, the Crusades by now having been outlawed by public resentment over the wars' excesses, their cost in human lives and in taxes. But the pope still believed he could conquer lands, take control of resources and build his authority. If not all Christendom, he would control the empire of emperors, the Roman world.

The twelfth century had seen an explosion of the new—new art, new forms of spirituality, new cathedrals and new governments. By the end of the thirteenth century, the creation of so much novelty had caused huge difficulties in diversity and urbanization. New schools of thought and religious practices triggered countermovements; new jobs and ways of life created perplexing choices. Big institutions were built to contain the fear social changes had brought. Nation-states were developed to balance diversity; spirituality was tempered in magnificent basilicas; guilds set controls on the ownership of wealth. At the head of the chain was the power of powers, the pope. Laws were no longer judged by the kings of Europe but by the vicar of Rome. The pope was the court of last resort.

Boniface built the papal bureaucracy to the point at which he and his staff were writing 50,000 letters a year voicing opinions on cases before their court, five times the number of his predecessor. Increasingly people brought conflicts before the pontiff, the highest court in western Europe. Boniface took advantage of these disputes to increase his power.

Defeated in his desire to launch a new crusade, Boniface turned his interest to Florence, which he wanted to see under the control of the Black Guelfs, the party of the church. This was what had put him at odds with Dante and his faction of the Ghibelline-like Guelfs, the party of imperial aspirations. Boniface sent in his papal troops led by Charles of Valois who reached Florence in November 1301. Riots began when the nobleman Corso Donati rode into the city to challenge Charles with armed troops of his own, throwing open the prisons, stealing, killing and finally prevailing. Donati sent Charles south after fining him 24,000 florins or nearly ten million dollars. Blacks set fire to the homes of their enemies, the Whites, and in a final gesture had salt strewn over the ruins, a symbolic act reminiscent of the Romans at Carthage, when they poured salt over the conquered lands so the defeated could grow nothing and thus be rendered dependent on their Roman overlords.

At the beginning of 1300, when Boniface renewed hostilities against Florence, he demanded that three of his opponents be turned over to him for justice. The city responded by electing the most prominent of these, "the corrupt but astute" Lapo Salterelli, to the high office of prior of the Republic. Boniface threatened an Inquisition and issued the *Unam Sanctam,* in which he declared: "The Roman pope has been selected by God as the judge of both the living and the dead, and has been granted all power, both in heaven and on earth. He rules above both kings and kingdoms . . . above all mortals, he holds his power as a prince. . . ."

That seemed to work. Dante, who respected the pope's authority on matters of spiritual salvation, not on political issues, believed in the new craft of negotiation. Reason and the desire for order would bring peace to Florence. The mission to Rome in 1301 in which Dante took part was meant to secure an understanding between the *caput mundi* and its sister city. Dante and Boniface met in Rome. Dante wished to discuss plans for peace in Florence. Boniface would not do so. Instead, he advised him to behave more humbly because, he said, at that very hour his city had been handed over to the opposing party of Black Guelfs. The lion had attacked. In a short time, Dante's political career and his life in Florence would be over.

Boniface's ambitions were to burn themselves out. From exile in the dark woods, Dante paid attention to the pope's unfolding fate. Boniface had forbidden Philip the Fair, of France, his sworn enemy, to tax the clergy, and Philip in turn prohibited the export of gold, silver and precious stones, blocking a major source of papal revenue. Philip's armies entered the papal bedroom at midnight on the Vigil of the Blessed Virgin's Nativity, September 7, 1303. Infatuated by his own majesty, Boniface left his room unguarded. At the first sound of alarm, he called his loyal servants to help him dress in his papal robes. Sitting on his throne, crucifix in hand, he met his enemies in silence, exactly as the Senators of old Rome had faced the wild soldiery of Gaul. The standoff lasted three days. The pope was denied food and drink. He was nearly eighty years old, weak but defiant as he watched his palace plundered—nothing was left but bare walls and the throne on which he was sitting. To humiliate him further, he was propped up on a wild horse with his face to the tail and led through the streets around the pope's summer palace at Anagni, a tiny mountain village south of Rome. In a last-ditch effort, Boniface dusted off the inquisitorial bull in which he declared himself chosen by God to lead the people. Philip's lieutenant threw it into the fire. But a copy was smuggled out of the palace. It excited public response in Boniface's favor, and he was rescued by the people, who scattered the invaders. He was taken back to Rome and the Vatican, and three days later he died. Dante condemned Philip's actions and will side with Boniface in *Purgatorio* 20.

What had Boniface's stupendous hunger gotten him? Hungry, barely standing, he walked to the marketplace and begged, "If there be any good woman who would give me alms of wine and bread, I would bestow upon her God's blessing and mine." The shock and humiliation killed him. Witnesses reported that his last act was that of gnawing his hands to the bone when he suffered his final death agonies.

In *Inferno,* Dante condemned Boniface for simony, or selling favors. He condemns all such traders in Circle 8, site of the *Malebolge*—the evil ditches, or the open tombs (Canto 10) of the fraudulent (26) and malicious who float in a river of excrement (18). They are assigned to depths according to their mistakes at love. In one ditch are the panderers and seducers—"the honey-tongued" with their dishonest lovers' wiles (18.91). "From every mouth a sinner's leg" sticks out. But there is one dead soul the flames can barely cover: the pope lies for eternity in the circle of

Hell below the flatterers who call evil good and good evil, their feet licked by flames.

> ... *"Se' tu già costì ritto,*
> *se' tu già costì ritto, Bonifazio?. ..."*

> "Are you there already, Boniface? Are you there
> already?"

(19.52–53ff.; trans. Ciardi)

One of Boniface's predecessors mistakes Dante for the pope who once satisfied himself on other people's hunger. This is a comedy of devils, each accusing the other, as Dante himself was accused by Boniface of barratry. Dante won't condescend to look at him. Boniface is not dead in 1300, the year in which the events of *Inferno* are set. But Dante evokes him in Hell, as if his soul were already owned by the devil when the poet met his condemner.

A statue of Boniface stands in Bologna, both a symbol and a caricature: a papal crown was stolen by soldiers in the French occupation. His right hand which once held two keys of precious metal—the Keys to the Kingdom—also stolen, now seem to make an empty gesture. The hands are surprisingly delicate, with long and tapered fingers, in contrast to his determined chin and massive jaw. The record states that he had large and forceful teeth.

> *la vista che m'apparve d'un leone.*
> *Questi parea che contra me venisse*
> *con la test' alta e con rabbiosa fame,*
> *sì che parea che l'aere ne tremesse.*

... a lion seemed to have come upon me with head erect, and
furious hunger; so that the air seemed to tremble around
him ...

(*Inferno* 1.46–48; amalgam of translations)

Two hundred years later, the great Dantista Niccolò Machiavelli
will read about Boniface and be thunderstruck. He will say that
nature had created unsatisfiable desire in man, but Fortune se-
verely limits that appetite. Power is an expedient, but it is not an
ambition he, Niccolò, can conjure in himself. It is the curse of man
to have such hunger, satisfy it, and have it flare up again. How can
one satisfy desire, ever? The question will plague Machiavelli, who
shoves the burden onto the republic to satisfy ambition. For Dante,
this path was not an option. If attaining the salvation of *Paradiso*
appears a probable goal in the poet's mind now in the years of writing *Inferno*, no one knows.

The death of Boniface on October 11, 1303, marks the beginning of the victory of nationalism over supernaturalism. Politics
will overtake the spiritual in its power over men and women and
social institutions. But Dante will create a synthesis of politics and
spirit in which he tries to stop the power of the sword from
reasserting itself against the magic of the word. Depicting the
emptiness of Boniface's worldly desires, Dante will stand against
the gathering social tide.

... *una lupa, che di tutte brame*
sembiava carca ne la sua magrezza,
e molte genti fé già viver grame

. . . a wolf that looked so full of all cravings,
and has made many live in sorrow.

(1.49–51; amalgam)

Hunger took an even more insidious form in the wolf. Dante feared the wolf more than the lion, because the wolf's appetite was more common to man and more insidious than the lion's extravagant desires. Wolfish hunger manifests itself as restlessness—desire beyond hunger. Such false desires make love impossible. Dante, especially in his reduced state, feared that man would be wolf to his fellow man. Only one person, Francis of Assisi, had followed these very roads in exile, one hundred years before Dante, betraying no hunger and free of ambition. He craved only love: Francis, who was poetry in Italy before Dante—and one who, legend insists, tamed a wolf.

In a world where there was one king and a mob of courtiers, St. Francis said he was one courtier in a mob of kings, a servant to all. He founded the humblest of the spiritual orders: he was not just a monk but a mendicant. Francis shunned desire so he could concentrate his energy on love as the end of desire. The ecclesiastical judge who declared Francis fit for sainthood wrote, "The devil may create miracles, but it takes a saint to live a sainted life." Few people can love poverty as Francis did. Love, he insisted, was the absence of desire.

There is an old Platonic myth created, it might seem, for Francis. Poverty, a disheveled creature, gate-crashes a party for the gods and tricks one of them, the rich and handsome Plenty, to sleep with her. Francis too had been a little god named Plenty. He had been swaddled in creature comforts. His rich father, arriving home a month after the boy's birth in 1181, changed the squalling infant's name from doughty John to Francis in honor of the French dandies with whom he so enjoyed doing business. Francis grew up true to his name. His mother would boast that her son went through money like a prince.

Then precisely in the middle of his life, like Dante, he had a conversion experience. His too came from a run-in with authority. Francis had sold expensive cloth for his father Pietro until a dream told him to fight in war. He left for battle in 1202, then fell ill and had another vision: to return home to serve the poor. Pietro, outraged to hear of his son's new vocation, locked him in a closet. His mother let him out. In a showdown, Pietro demanded back everything he'd given his son. Francis threw the money in his pockets and the clothes he was wearing in Pietro's face, announcing before their friends and neighbors, "My father is not the father of anyone at all."

Poverty married Plenty in Plato's myth and Francis did the same in life—both produced a child named Love, which Francis defines as charity, *caritas.* Francis's love was the love for every living thing, sentient and nonsentient alike and equally—popes, sultans and peasants, birds and bugs, fire and dust.

Dante too would speak to the dead, to fire, to dust clouds, and perhaps he would learn some of his method from Francis. Francis's secret is said to be that he never distinguished the forest from the trees. Every tree was an individual, and so he never saw people or things in generalizations. It is a kind of seeing that brooks no distinctions so prized by rationalists. The Latin word for "knowledge," *sapientia,* means the distinctions of the tongue, taste. In concentrating on each individual entity, Francis could hear or see in them the soul of perfection, the energy of God. That concentration required that he reject literacy and knowledge. Francis's most controversial position was in his defense of illiteracy. It was part of his poetry of living. Knowledge, he felt, depended on doubt, while faith—belief in the impossible— increased only by belief in absurdity.

It is said that Francis had the courage to see, not hide behind imagination—which made him a poet of life more than of the page. Francis achieved this ability to look and see what others missed by, paradoxically, blinding himself to knowledge, a lethal form of desire, he felt. By thus making submissive his natural human hubris, he believed he became infused with genius from a higher will.

Francis taught himself to bear a lot of reality. Going blind in his forties, he submitted to the only known remedy of the time: to cauterize the eyeballs, or burn them, unanesthetized, with a hot iron. When the brand was about to be applied, Francis spoke to the fire, something he often did: "Brother Fire, God made you beautiful and strong and useful. I pray that you be courteous with me." No wonder Dante began addressing the flames in Hell.

"If life is art, this is a masterpiece moment," Chesterton exclaimed. Francis lived one of his own poems. The flame embodied a number of souls: he remembered when the flame was a flower, a poppy with which Umbrian fields blaze in April. "When the shining thing returned to him in the shape of an instrument of torture, he addressed it by its nickname." *Brother Fire.* This is no ordinary brotherhood of the backslapping kind, Chesterton noted. "It's a camaraderie founded on courtesy," a loving friendship with everything, human and not. "People with such magnetism and self-belief exercise a tremendous power," he suggests.

The day he renounced his father, young Francis, naked, cold

and alone, exiled from home, walked into the woods, singing. A peasant, feeling sorry for him, gave him an old worn tunic of his own—"the color of a beast," Francis proudly said—and he tied it closed with a rope around his waist. Ten years later "that make-shift costume" was the habit of 5,000 men. A hundred years later, in that costume "they laid great Dante in the grave." Francis's brotherhood had grown and attracted, ironically, the best scholars of the late 1200s and early 1300s.

As they spread, Francis's views triggered a social revolution against the nightmare of hungry wolves in the dark forests. Since ancient Roman times, a householder believed his purpose was to increase his family's status, not decrease it. Francis defiantly called money "excrement." Love makes people do foolish things. Francis walked barefoot in snow, and gave his crumbs to the birds. Unlike the other great purists Socrates and Jesus, Francis considered poverty a pleasure, not a duty. His asceticism was the height of optimism. To the modern notion that "one who expects noth-ing can't be disappointed," Francis believed that "one who ex-pects nothing enjoys everything." The poverty he sought was the poverty of pride: "The less one thinks of oneself, the more one thinks of one's good luck." He roused the sons and daughters of rich families and poor alike to leave their homes and follow him into caves and under the starry skies. Poverty and ignorance built a tremendous following and made Francis the counselor of popes and sultans.

By Dante's time, Francis's brotherhood with its balance be-tween poverty and plenty will be challenged by Thomas Aquinas. Thomas will write the *Summa Theologica*, an encyclopedia of 21 volumes containing 38 treatises, raising 631 questions and offering 10,000 arguments, containing all that is known. Thomas will thank God not for ignorance, as the thin and starving Francis thanked God, but for the divine fullness of knowledge.

The bread Francis gathers in beggary only to scatter to the birds has changed its spiritual form by Dante's time. Bread acquires a rational basis: the new science of anatomy reveals that biologically, bread turns bile into blood. The new science of economics secularizes bread as money. In the early 1300s, businesses assert themselves in town life. They take the name "company," which literally means "with bread": *companie*. These superguilds will fatten populations, luring them often from churches and justice.

*

FRANCIS'S REPUDIATION OF all human desires and his own personal charisma greatly influenced Dante, but as always, Dante melded his influences. Dante argued for total authority for the empire and total poverty for the church. To him, poverty is power when combined with imperial power. Wherever poverty is not observed, cupidity drives out charity and justice. He came to believe that the church should own nothing and the emperor everything—so he cannot be bought. One should receive goods not as a possessor but as a dispenser of them. Francis was Christ's most faithful imitator, and Dante Francis's most faithful interpreter.

And anyway, what was there to want? "A monk should own nothing but his harp," Franciscans say, meaning that he should value nothing but his song. Francis sang his poetry to beg bread and to express his joy in being alive. This was "the practical side of asceticism." One had to be slim to pass through the bars of one's cage, and travel light to ride fast and far. One couldn't threaten to starve a person who was always striving to fast. He couldn't be ruined or reduced to poverty; he was already a beggar. One couldn't threaten him because "indignity was his only dignity."

While Francis has kept the wolf at bay, the only other creature he treats with more disdain is his "brother the Ass," his own body, which he ruined with fasting and a life as a perpetual exile on Umbrian roads. He dies at the age of forty-five, in the company of his brothers.

*

una lonza leggiera e presta molto,
che di pel macolato era coverta . . .

a leopard, light and very nimble,
covered with festive skin . . .

(*Inferno* 1.32–33; trans. Pinsky)

One more animal stands between Dante and the descent into Hell. That is the leopard, the most bedeviling creature. The leopard, at its best, is every "light love," as Ovid said.

Could Dante have seen the leopard flash in the story his friend Giotto told of Francis's life? Giotto's Francis is the Francis people love. The "Leopard" Francis is lovely to look at, with a solid human body, unstarved, full. That the young Giotto received the commission to paint Francis's life on the walls of Assisi in tableaus the size and height of a feature film screen was a coup, an economic windfall. The church was built on the saint's bones in 1228, two years after Francis's death. But Giotto was distinctly unlike Francis. The saint chased after poverty as avidly as Giotto pursued riches. At the time he was painting Francis's life on the walls of Francis's church, Giotto satirized "Holy Poverty." In one poem he wrote, he joked about the excesses of the Fratricelli, the radical Franciscans. From the time the work was complete, by 1296, Giotto priced his services as high as the most established master painters.

When he received the Assisi commission, Giotto was on his way to becoming one of the richest and most entrepreneurial artists of his time, not only taking on expensive commissions, but "banking" his resources: he rented out looms in his workshops to weavers, and sold his brushes and sketches. He bought land. He believed that poverty was the road to sin because it leads judges to commit errors. Only his painting was spare, praised as "pure and without ornament."

Giotto raised to a height the High Middle Ages' gradual attainment of the great modern notion that one can create one's own wealth by changing worthless goods and paper into costly objects. Giotto practiced his art brilliantly. Petrarch, in the years after Dante's death, will caution visitors against believing that the saint, Francis, was captured in the shadows Giotto painted on the walls of this churchly cave. The nature of hunger, for one, makes the times of the saint and the artist vastly different. By the time of Giotto's maturity, Heaven begins to seem farther away. Aristotle animates Thomas Aquinas's work. The physical world was being appreciated in a way it hadn't since Roman times. Before Giotto, no painter had painted the sky blue. When Michelangelo entered the great church of Assisi at the height of the Renaissance, a time even more robustly physical than the Middle Ages, he understood that the artist's magic had outdone the saint's.

Giotto did for Francis on fresco surfaces what Michelangelo would do in sculpture in Carrara's finest marble: he made observers move to take in his figures, to change their perspective. In the church of Assisi, people wonder still at the saint whose only tenement in life had been a ragged cloth which barely covered him. Now he was housed in this imposing structure, looking as if he had eaten the birds who had feasted on the bread he shared. Francis had believed that to build a church is not to pay for it, not even with someone else's money. The way to build a church is to build it by begging people for stones, reversing the parable: a beggar who begs not for bread but for stones.

But when he saw Giotto's depiction of the death of Saint Francis, Michelangelo wept. In that scene, Francis lies prone, his followers kissing his cold hands and feet. One's attention focuses on the kissing of his hands and feet. No one paints a kiss like Giotto, and no one could paint the lack of desire in a kiss better than he could. Kisses so transcendent and loving they need nothing. Kisses without desire.

*

THE ASCETICS AND aesthetes change places. Craftsmen and guildsmen, the forerunners of bankers and organization men, vie with heroes who gave it all up for love, who welcomed poverty and suffering because it took them deeper into the mysteries of knowledge. The old heroes don't want comfort, they want adventure. Nobility is their grail. The enormous project of church-building engages the new artists' guilds. They gather according to their skills. Freemasons were the bricklayers, and the secrets of their artistry were breached on punishment of death. Guilds were institutions in restraint of trade, strongest in Italy where the old Roman institutions were best preserved. The word, mysteries, from the medieval Latin meaning "guilds," is onomatopoeic. Mmmm-ystery: keep one's lips sealed. The greater guilds spread throughout Europe.

In the year Dante is laid in his grave in a Franciscan tunic there appears a book, *Secreta Fidelium Crucis* (The Secrets of the Faithful of the Cross). It is the first work on political and commercial economy. Its author proposed not a crusade, but a commercial and maritime blockade of Egypt. The subject is treated fantastically and the transition from religious ideas to those of trade are awkwardly managed. A great crusade is beginning, but of a thoroughly new kind. Men are not going in quest of the Grail but in search of sugar or cinnamon. This hero of the modern world risks for the gain of a sequin as much as St. Francis risked for the poor. The new crusader finds his Jerusalem everywhere.

The new religion—wealth, faith in gold—had its pilgrims, its monks, its martyrs, who dare and who suffer, just as the others dared and suffered. They too watch, fast, practice self-denial. They pass their best years on dangerous roads, in distant countries. Francis's order and Giotto's means have married.

Aligheri would become Dante by synthesizing the warring elements. He would combine the power of the ruling pope, the vision of wealth that distorts purity, and the self-sacrificial effort at extreme poverty. He will achieve a balance: he must become the poet of penury that is riches, massive money that impoverishes, power that is overthrown. He must become the outcast who attains a crown. In that synthesis is his power. He achieves it by particular means, like Francis, by his example, and like Giotto, by the story he tells.

★

WHAT T. S. ELIOT learned from Dante, and what Dante must have learned early in exile, is the quality of "lived" experience. According to Eliot scholar Lyndall Gordon, "Eliot found that if he cast his mind into the flux between different viewpoints, and held them momentarily together, he could sometimes discern a 'half object,' a composite of the viewpoints which yet transcended them. When he made the necessary intuitive leap, he discovered his power to see 'the real future of an imaginary present.' The language . . . suggests a quasi religious experience: a pilgrimage into the space between two worlds. Prophetic power is the reward of an 'act of faith.'"

To live like a visionary in the dangerous space between two worlds was to court madness. But to fall back into the net of the material world and to live enmeshed in its artificial customs and beliefs was to risk the gift for sublime knowledge. Dante helped Eliot see the connection between the medieval Christian Inferno and modern life. Both the poet and his reader have to plumb the depths of Hell and bear the ordeals of Purgatory to reach the love that frees one of desire. Love becomes the basis of creativity. Love as the habit of genius is Dante's invention, his miraculous synthesis.

Francis's love—*caritas,* charity—is not sufficient to assure one's move up the mountain and into Paradise in the culture in which bread is not just spirit but also money. A different kind of love, *amor,* which is intimate and spiritual will do that. *Amor* is not charity. It is divine love that is individual, as in the feeling of a parent for a child or a lover for a beloved. In *Inferno*, Dante will see love as an enslaving passion, desire run amok. But he will transcend the mistakes of love made by Boniface and even by Francis, Giotto and others. He will find that a person enslaved by love dies; a person liberated by love acts. To Danteans, there come to mind the words of Gabriel García Márquez's hero: "It is as if you had been given back to me again after you died." After the encounter with the beasts, Dante's own lover, Beatrice, will return with a promise to guide him upward only if he agrees to make the trip down. He goes.

Dantean Pilgrimages

Dante's pilgrimage begins in Hell, across the River Acheron, where "no soul in Grace"—Dante is an exception—"ever comes." "Master," he says to his guide Virgil, "I long to know who these souls are," and why "their lamentation stuns the very air." "They have no hope of death," Virgil answers. Their torments are continual.

> And in their blind and unattaining state
> their miserable lives have sunk so low
> that they must envy every other fate.
>
> (3.43–45; trans. Ciardi)

In the sounds uttered and silent, Dante can hear both kinds of cries:

the tear-soaked ground gave out a sigh of wind
   that spewed itself in flame on a red sky,
   and all my shattered senses left me. Blind,

like one whom sleep comes over in a swoon,
I stumbled into darkness and went down.

                (3.129–33; trans. Ciardi)

Eliot's pilgrimage begins with the hope of completing this most difficult task: "to force [himself] awake." He thought to do this through marriage. But his first wife, Vivienne, lapsed into schizophrenia. London, to which he had emigrated, was a site of urban despair. His friend Virginia Woolf called the literary marketplace "the Underworld." "Eliot's childhood had been empty of beauty," according to biographer Gordon. "He had been brought up to see goodness as practical, and to take the line of self-interest, not redemption, in a code of rewards and punishments. This was his secret inferno, an emotional stage which had to be traversed before he could be worthy of a genuine awakening." Eliot said, in 1922, as he began to study *Inferno* again, this time not for an undergraduate thesis, but as a life project: "It's interesting to cut yourself to pieces once in a while, and wait to see if the fragments will sprout."

Eliot began reading Dante in a whole new light: not to expose the speaker, but to create the reader—himself. He reached through the *Comedy* to "the sermon that haunts it." There, he said, he found a new psychology: Once there existed "a psychological habit, the trick of which we have forgotten, but as good as any of our own. We have nothing but dreams, and we have forgotten that seeing visions—a practice now relegated to the aberrant and uneducated—was once a more significant, interesting, and disciplined kind of dreaming. We take it for granted that our dreams spring from below: possibly the quality of our dreams suffers in consequence."

Through Dante, the world became, for Eliot, round once more, the depths lost their threat, and the darkness became pure surface on which he could walk. Hell and its sufferings, which he shared, although completely incomprehensible on one level, seemed to have a solution.

Eliot's was a far different experience from that of the poet John Keats when he traveled to the Scottish highlands with Dante's account of the afterlife in his knapsack. Keats had his share of torment: a poor mother, dependent on her son; poverty; the first signs of tuberculosis; an agonizing love life. He was to die at the age of twenty-six. On what he hoped was a walk that would alter his fortunes, he read *Inferno*. But the reality of Dante's Hell and the highlands' Heaven as he tested them was as doubtful as the earth he could not see in the thick mist. Nature was a mirror of the worlds of intellect he could not penetrate. There was no revelation, no loss of self for a greater vision. All Keats found at the top of his mountain was confusion, disappointment and bad comedy. As he wrote to his brother Tom, "There is not a more fickle thing than the top of a Mountain."

Keats had the right instinct but the wrong method for exploiting Dante. There are no shortcuts to *Paradiso*, nor any shortcuts to relief. *Inferno* has to be experienced. One has to bring the bottom along as one climbs. The way up, Dante tells us, is the way down.

CHAPTER 4

The Ogre of the Brotherhood

Ora sen va per un secreto calle,
tra 'l muro de la terra e li martiri,
lo mio maestro, e io dopo le spalle.

We go by a secret path along the rim
of the dark city, between the wall and the torments.
My master leads me, and I follow him.

(*Inferno* 10.1–3; trans. Ciardi)

ALTHOUGH GENIUS WAS BORN IN FLORENCE, it was not made there. For that, one's path wound through Bologna.

One hundred miles from Florence but more importantly one hundred years ahead of it, young men born far away were crossing the snowy Alps and the marshlands, 10,000 strong. They were being drawn to Bologna to work their way down the path of learning—from knowledge to discovery, arriving at last at the body, the sexual organs and the senses: the most corrupted of the levels of wisdom.

One of Bologna's best and brightest arrivals, Florence-born Guido Cavalcanti, is now relegated to a footnote in Danteana, a bit of an embarrassment really, because it is said of him that he found a route to Paradise shorter than the whole long heretical *Comedy* maintains is necessary. He believed that God is dead and that divine secrets are for the taking. He was an aristocrat, a knight without a knighthood, but also a Don Quixote minus the parody. Lorenzo de' Medici, Ezra Pound, Percy Shelley and others have identified with the ambitious Guido and found themselves in trouble. Proximity to the myth of Guido makes one too confident and opinionated, too quick to believe oneself a poet, which Guido defined as a discoverer, not an inventor, whose secrets he found in pleasure, the shortcut, not the longer route of error and suffering. Critics typically discourse on how Dante learned his worldview from Aquinas and the schoolmasters who in turn debate on such matters as where in the soul rage resides. But Cavalcanti took a different route to genius. He went through Bologna—the center of cold logic and oriental mysteries so hot that people were being burned for reading them.

Guido is a poet with a mission—not just to entertain or delight. He believes it to be the most important mission of the thirteenth and fourteenth centuries—to discover the nature of genius, based on the supposition—developed by Saint Augustine in the fourth century A.D.—that God too is a poet, a writer who has such an amazing way that his words become not just breath forgotten the minute they are uttered, but things more real and true than matter.

*

IN FLORENCE, IT was possible to learn the basics—grammar, rhetoric, logic, arithmetic, geometry, music, astronomy: "the seven liberal arts"—but Bologna held the secrets. Bologna was nicknamed *la città grossa*, fat city. Whatever one wanted, Bologna was the place to find it.

It is an ironic scrap of linguistic fate that the word Bologna has become slang for "concoction," for "pure baloney," from the sausage invented there: mortadella, which is the most delicious meal of the deadest part of the pig—bones with bristle and hoofs thrown in. Bologna sausage is not pure even by sausage standards; nor is the learning in Bologna. The other renowned product of this beautiful grey city with streets that seem to turn in on their secrets is the University of Bologna, unique in the medieval world, an institution run by its students. The University of Paris had been the center of learning for more than a century, but recently it had been run with an iron fist by its masters to keep the students from destroying the city by raping and stealing and mistaking themselves for the gods they weren't supposed to be reading about in "pagan" literature.

The would-be Zeuses took freely whatever they wanted. But what really brought the curtain down on Paris and the aims of these young men was Peter Abelard. The brilliant young Abelard had given up his father's fortune to serve his own quest for learning, but he defied his Parisian masters on how to study God. One ought to study church scholarship and authority, he believed, not merely justify its assertions. He developed the method we call deductive thinking. He subjected religion to philosophy, and in fact coined the word "theology." That act of defiance against the church, and not his love affair with Héloïse as many believe, is what earned him charges of calumny and a nighttime raid by his teachers to cut off his testicles. The message from the masters of Paris was chilling: logic would not be welcome there. Rules and procrustean restrictions came to dominate the Paris curriculum. The sons of rich families stopped arriving in the Left Bank.

Bologna picked up the slack. In Bologna, the inmates ran the asylum. The students took charge of the university: they set the rules and hired the faculty. They had the capacity for this job: they were older than their counterparts in Paris—many of them already practicing doctors and lawyers. Besides, what difference did a little hell make? This was a city in which one could stab one's political opponent openly on the streets. And the message issuing forth was that Hell, and Heaven, were lies. *Bononia Docet,* reads the inscription over the school's coat of arms. Bologna teaches. It was the center of the most radical, newest thinking in the middle and late 1200s. The city had dubbed itself "Liberty," which in Latin shares a root with "licentious."

We don't know the year, but Cavalcanti arrived at the University of Bologna for a taste of dangerous knowledge. On a route that might have made him the most original voice of his day, he had to cross the line drawn, uncertainly, over knowledge and propriety. Shaky the line may be, but cross it he would.

Events were changing rapidly in the last decade of the 1200s, and the nature of reality was coming into focus as never before in the Middle Ages. The new world was not America or some star at the end of a telescope. Not yet. It was the body.

In the north—the students leaving the University of Paris, and from the centers of Arab learning—people were gradually growing accustomed to using their eyes. But it would be another hundred years before they would actually trust them. Lenses of the kind used in eyeglasses were invented in 1300, but they were not turned into eyeglasses until the late fifteenth century because it was thought that appearances—literally, the way things looked— were deceiving. People trusted instead the inner meaning of things. They favored writers who made the most appeal to the mind and least to the eye. Now, the Arab translators in Bologna left behind the historians and the poets tortured by feelings of the spirit. The tragic dramatists were of no use to them. Nor was Homer. Instead, they took to the writings about natural science and medicine.

These texts represented the missing pieces, and young radicals like Guido devoured them. It was no great effort to imagine the immortality of the soul. It is a heroic effort to imagine the resurrection of the body. On Judgment Day, are you returned to your lusty, lustrous adolescent body, or to that withered frame you said goodbye to as you died? Guido wanted to know.

Bologna made the body preeminent. Doctors were developing the new art of autopsy, opening the body to decode its mysteries. Bologna's greatest claim to fame is that human anatomy was first taught there in the early fourteenth century. The first autopsies were performed there. For all its boldness, however, there were limits to physical acceptance: the first woman to teach at a university taught at Bologna, astonishing in itself, but Novella d'Andrea had to lecture concealed behind a curtain. She was said to be terribly attractive.

Medicine was a controversial path, which may be why Guido loved it. Opening the body, plumbing its secrets brought physicians into conflict with the doctors of the soul. Little was known about the body until the brilliant Arab literature was brought west during the Crusades.

Averroës, the twelfth-century Arab commentator on the scientific works of Aristotle, argued that if the soul dies with the body and pleasure is only a state of the here and now, then Heaven and Hell are lies. Averroism swept literate Tuscany beginning in 1240, and in 1277, Aristotelian propositions began to be banned from the schools, surfacing only among a band of scholars known as "radical Aristotelians." In just a few years, a doctor, Peter of Abano, will be sentenced to trial for defying this order. His patients will protect him, but two years later the courts will arrest him, and this time he will avoid trial only by dying. This won't, however, be enough to spare him. The powers of Florence will make every effort to seize his corpse and burn it. Not finding it, thanks to friends who have hidden it, they will burn Peter in effigy.

Punishment for reading Aristotle or Averroës's commentary, *The Destruction of the Destruction,* was very much in the air in the 1290s. And so the Tuscan bookworms whose greatest joy had been the beautiful *Fioretti* of St. Francis suddenly found themselves with Guido in the groves of philosophy. "Brother sun," "sister moon and the stars," the short, simple, ecstatic rhythms which were the work of Francis met the new knowledge of the body. This was the source of Guido's fame. Guido introduced into self-knowledge "that new style in which the eyes and the heart and the soul have separate voices of their own and converse together. God became interesting, and speculation, with open eyes and a rather didactic voice, is boon companion to the bard," Ezra Pound exulted from his perspective as the savior of the Guido myth in the early 1900s.

Guido's tutor in Bologna was the world-famous physician-philosopher Taddeo Alderotti, who taught the belief that the soul is generated by the semen that makes the body. Souls, the Egyptian Ptolemy had taught in the second century, were splinters of stars—fragments of heavenly light that fell to earth, and got dirty on the descent into earth's atmosphere. The tarnish comprised human characteristics, such as lust (if these bits of starlight drifted too close to the planet of love, Venus) or anger if they got smudged on warlike Mars. Bodies had hardly any substance at all.

This is what the science of the time considered "knowledge." Alderotti said that a poet does not choose his words. A poet expresses the alterations taking place in his body. Words are a bodily event. When there is a sighlike sound in poetry, it is meant to discharge the pressure in the heart. Writing poetry is an internal effort toward vision. So Guido learned that the intellect stands in the same relation to the soul as the senses to the mind. Where then is the "beyond"? "Where is the border, this place where ecstasy is not a whirl or a madness of the senses, but a glow arising from the exact nature of the perception?" asked Ezra Pound. Not only where is this ecstasy felt most, but how does one attain its mesmerizing excitement?

And would this excitement be the real thing: Paradise? Right here, in the body? But how would the body know perfection—this vulnerable, animal mass which is all desire and no direction? Wasn't beauty the province, almost exclusively, of the soul?

Such a route was important to follow because it seemed to lead to the Code: Genius—the formula by which one could live as a god.

The Code, the poets supposed, could be discovered as if it were genomic letters that spelled something readable, or more than readable—something poetic, the solution to the mysteries of life.

Nature in the thirteenth century was not a separate category of thought; it was God's writing. If you knew the sequence of letters and words in God's style, you could write the word "rose" and a rose would bud before you. It sounds outlandish, but this is essentially what genomic scientists now believe. The Code *had* to be cracked, because the end of knighthood had arrived. There was no new order; everything was up for grabs in this rush of the new, giving rise to unsettled conditions. The second half of the thirteenth century was one in which the earlier ideals of knights and nobility were crumbling. Dante stresses harmony in the *Comedy*, but there are intimations of a world of lost directions, of angst, of failing nerve. The Crusades were over. Acre was the last Christian city to fall to Muslim control in 1291. This last fortress fell with apocalyptic intensity. Fear and uncertainty were growing. In the atmosphere of heightened religious practice, individualism and growing freedom, the solution seemed to lie in proximity to God.

Guido and soon Dante considered the most important mission to be their own: Can one produce a soul worthy of the angels? To put it differently: the hero was still incomplete, even after centuries of adventurous turns and a great deal of poetry. Aeneas and King Arthur were heroic characters; Virgil and other poets were brilliant creators of heroes, but in themselves lesser men. Could there be a poet with the attributes of his best creations, who would not die but who would live at full tilt in his mortal years and later in people's souls, bringing his visions to life in others?

Of course, it would be a poet who would break such a code. Poets were priests without the cumbersome theology. Poets do not give us doctrine but their own gradual illumination. Even a king of the time, Enzio, eventually thrown into jail in Bologna, was visited in his cell by students who wanted to hear him read his verse. Enzio, the favorite son of Frederick II, Holy Roman emperor and then king of Sicily, valued his poetry enough to mention it in his will along with his gold and his unmarried daughters. How far we have come, or how far we have fallen, depends on one's point of view: The *Summa Theologica* of St. Thomas was, in its time, a manual for the use of university students. Today, where are the students who would be capable of assimilating all, or any, of its twenty-one volumes?

Love was the secret, and not love as we see it in movies today—as heat or sexual passion, but love as light, as the key to revelation. The body was the ladder to wisdom. One is never sure with Guido whether his interpretations are philosophical or erotic or a mixture of the two. What seems to underlie his erotic daring and philosophic vainglory is his overweening pride. In this, he will clash with Dante, who is still at the time of their friendship, a decade before Dante's exile, uncertain as Hamlet, his Etruscan nose buried in books and caught in self-deliberation. Dante sought to domesticate his erotic feelings, Guido to bask in them.

*

SUCH THINGS WOULD come between Dante and Guido over seventeen years of friendship. But perhaps the most divisive rift would be the definition of love as the means to genius. For Guido, love was *loves*. It was a "disruption"—a heightening of the brain's activities and bodily emotions. For Dante, it was love—one, singular and transcendent object of unswerving dedication. The energy put into that love, Dante believed, would make him the source for justice and beauty, and who needs more to realize perfection. It would make possible the ultimate shift, from ethics to aesthetics, from moral calls based on narrowing judgments to choices based on widening experiences of beauty. Before elegance became a principle of physics, it was Dante's.

There were many reasons for Dante and Guido to fall out. But what happened at the end of their friendship is telling. The most important event in the friendship of Guido and Dante is Guido's death.

The year is 1290. Dante is twenty-five, Guido thirty-four. Beatrice Portinari dies. Dante has loved her since he saw her when she was a child of nine. He has kept his distance from her, but death is too great a gulf even for him. He suffers a breakdown. It is not clear what happens to him. Guido has been his friend for eight years. They had met when Dante at eighteen wrote a sonnet saying he dreamed of Beatrice eating his flaming heart and asked what this meant. Guido is already famous. When Boniface said in the 1290s that his interest in Florence had to do with the fact that besides the four elements of earth, air, fire and water recognized by contemporary philosophy, Florence contained a fifth—the Florentine genius—he was speaking not about Dante, but about Cavalcanti. Guido wrote Dante a sonnet explaining this dream as one of a love about to die.

Guido's loves are easy come, easy go. In that spirit, he confronts the grieving Dante. "Afflicted soul," he reprimands, what are you doing thinking "vile thoughts"? Dante appears not to follow Guido's advice to shake free of his bereavement, as Guido expects him to. Perfection in a dead woman? A ridiculous thought to Guido, but not to Dante. It sounds as if Guido washes his hands of his friend: "And now I care not," Guido writes him, "since thy life is baseness." Guido leaves Florence on a pilgrimage to the holy house of Galicia, a stronghold of Christian Spain.

Impatience is a quality Dante will situate in Hell as a perversion of love. What one wants, one waits for and earns. Guido's thoughts move on a different plane: one creates Hell for one's enemies, not for oneself. Guido's logic doesn't allow him to see possible moves. Logicians discount wrong moves automatically. Less gifted people plod forward from error to error, taking the long route because they can't see the solution right before them. Is that how Dante looks to Guido, like a plodder?

Guido gets only as far as Toulouse when Corso Donati, his political enemy, attempts to assassinate him. He returns to Florence in 1296. No sooner is he back than he is attacked by Corso in the streets of Florence, provoked perhaps by some affront. For the long, ensuing turmoil, leaders of both Guelf and Ghibelline factions, White and Black, are exiled to restore peace. Guido is sent with the White Guelf faction to Sarzana.

In 1299, Dante, thirty-four, as second alderman, or senator, of the republic of Florence, votes on Guido's exile and signs the decree. Even by Florentine standards, the summer of 1300 arrived early and turned vengefully muggy. Ink was slow to dry on the new parchments, miraculously white, so much better than the yellowed skins long in use. Documents drawn on the new material were the pride of Tuscan notaries, who left them out, hanging like art, to dry in a rare passing breeze.

Perhaps in that summer the swamps were especially noxious. The Black Plague, which would begin in 1348 and destroy half the population of Europe before it exhausted itself sometime around 1380, fed on swamps. In Sarzana, an errant, early bug bit Cavalcanti, who suffered a malarial fever and died. The most celebrated poet of his day, he left two children and a vacuum in Florentine society. He was famous not only as a poet, but also as a thinker, a conversationalist, a person with ideas. The only bad luck in Guido's charmed life was to have been born in the same century as Dante Aligheri.

His death is so sudden that when Guido is brought back for burial, the ink on the decree of his exile may not yet have been dry. *Contrapasso*: counterstrike, one of the fundamental principles in the *Inferno*. It is an act of divine justice that redirects the essence of a crime back against the perpetrator. Dante suffers the ultimate justice. The law of retribution is the only law in Hell. Reciprocal wounds bind victim to criminal. Dante comes upon Bertrand de Born, knight and troubadour, who lived in the years 1140–1215. Bertrand had instigated a quarrel between Henry II of England and his son, Prince Henry. That offense requires Bertrand to carry his head by its hair, separated from his body, swinging like a lantern to light his dark path.

> "... *Perch' io parti' così giunte persone,*
>   *partito porto il mio cerebro, lasso!,*
>   *dal suo principio ch'è in questo troncone.*

> ... since I parted those who should be one

> in duty and in love, I bear my brain
> divided from its source within this trunk;
> and walk where my evil turns to pain,

> *Così s'osserva in me lo contrapasso."*

74

an eye for an eye to all eternity:
this is the law of Hell observed in me.

(*Inferno* 28.139–42; trans. Ciardi)

This sinner begs to be remembered. A roundabout confession on Dante's part of guilt for having separated Cavalcanti from the world of the living?

Is Dante's action murder? The Greek tragedians have a word for this crime: *hamartia*. They define it as an innocent act with colossal consequences. A son going on a trip mistakenly kills his father en route. A young man marries an older woman, and she turns out to be his mother. Accepting a dinner invitation to his brother's home, a man finds he has eaten his children cooked in the stew. Innocence, the ancient poets tell us, is dangerous; it can attract the wolves.

Cavalcanti's death has an eerie, haunting effect on Dante: he begins to live the dead man's life. Perhaps for reasons of guilt, Dante may think so often about Guido that he becomes him. Obsessions are deadly mirrors. The psalmist warns, "We become what we behold." Dante will suffer an exile; he too will die of a fever from a mosquito bite, also in a trek through a swamp. And many of Guido's ideas will live as his own. It was Guido who first spoke of Paradise as a career for the visionary here on earth, Guido who used poetry as a form of philosophy. The form of the *Commedia* itself may have been Guido's inspiration. *Inferno* was provoked by this line of Guido's poetry: "The place where I found people each of whom grieved overly of Love." It was Guido who suggested to Dante that he use popular speech and wean himself from Virgil's Latin. Dante does so in the *Comedy*. Dante will write again in Latin after he begins the *Comedy*: *De Monarchia* is the most celebrated of his Latin works. Nevertheless, Dante places Virgil in Limbo in the *Comedy*, hardly fitting for the master he loved unequivocally: "Without hope," says Virgil of the anxieties of Limbo, "we live on in desire" (*Inferno* 4.42). Dante makes Virgil his guide, but not an unerring one.

Guido had used his connections to get Dante a job in politics, where he had reached the level of alderman. He had introduced him to the aristocracy, which Dante took advantage of, yet berated. He had tried to impress upon him that the soul didn't consider the body a dying animal to drag around, and Averroës's cherished belief that the only people incapable of a sin are those who have already committed it.

Does Dante indeed will Cavalcanti's demise? The end of Guido is the end of lyric poetry for Dante. The two carried out an ongoing conversation of nearly two decades in sonnets, but there is evidence that Dante began pulling away from Guido's powerful influence by the end of *Vita Nuova*. Love poems soon after the *Vita* lose their meaning for Dante. He is thrust to the threshold of epic thinking. He is brought to questioning the very foundation of the poet's purpose: confronting whether language and truth are compatible. What is true in any action? When we say "I love you," do we feel love? Does our beloved? In the soul and in the body? How is one to convey truth so another receives its full value, not hypocritical or—to use a word from another time—unconscious intentions? Can language bear the weight of truth? These are questions of how to be understood, or "read," in the deepest sense—the quest, at heart, of politicians, philosophers, generals, anyone for whom another's life is on the line. Lovers too.

*

DANTE WILL MAKE hell a place of multiform loves, perversions of love, mistakes of love—as if accepting Guido's inspiration while at the same time denying Guido's influence. Dante's Hell will have more in common with the Marquis de Sade than with the Gospel of John. He will come to see that everything wrong with a person's vision has to do with energy wasted on the wrong or diverse passions. Genius is not found in desires, but in the choice of one desire, pursued against all else.

Guido's death fuels new questions in Dante in a way the young scholars in Paris or Bologna never imagined. Dante's search for happiness will take him to realms that intrude on other mysteries than the body, to a different kind of self-understanding. Dante saw the soul after death. Guido's vision, even of the body, was peculiarly blind. Boccaccio tells a story in *The Decameron* that Guido could become totally unaware when absorbed in chess. As a prank, a boy once nailed down his coattails to the bench while playing, scrunching up several folds of the cloth and driving the nail through. Guido felt nothing.

*

EVEN NOW IN the twenty-first century, Bolognese students rush around in the rain, their heads hooded like Fausts eager to strike a bargain with the devil for all of human knowledge. The university is no longer at the pinnacle of knowledge. The city is full of tombs of saints and kings who look as if they know more than they will ever tell, and the two leaning towers, like most of the caprices of the Middle Ages, seem a riddle that begs for an answer, a stupefying mystery, perhaps even a joke if one believes the whole world is a comedy.

There are other riddles that Bologna can't help us answer. One is the Pygmalion myth turned dark: We know that Dante is often characterized as devoutly religious. It is an interpretation that misses the all-important aspects of his dark eroticism. The evidence that Dante was not as pious as he seems in those self-righteous portraits of him arise from two pieces of evidence. One is his adolescent love for the nine-year-old girl, Beatrice. The second is the strange bond of love and faith he entered into with Guido, who is so quickly discounted.

These are two men connected by their conflict and their fanaticism, by a spiritual and poetic field. When the philosopher Hegel, a Dantista, said in the late 1800s that "we create each other," he meant somewhat abstractly what the medieval love poets took literally. In love, people create each other. We are not courageous or tall or fat or shy except as other people see us. Hegel dubbed this "the master/slave parable." Guido and Dante—teacher and apprentice—were also master and slave. Guido was dependent on Dante's admiration, Dante on Guido's guidance. When master and slave become dependent on each other, freedom becomes a life-or-death struggle, usually symbolic. To get free, the master must kill the slave, or vice versa. People don't typically die to get free of these forceful relationships; they just don't return calls, as philosopher Robert Solomon says. Death, such as it is, comes from mortification. But then poets are literal about things.

They will not meet again, not even in Hell. Dante will bid farewell to arms in *Inferno*. He will, with Guido's death, discover that missing in the brotherhood they shared was the heroic imagination that finds pleasure in peace. What he will discover in Guido's death is that logic does not carry truth. In logic, one can argue one thing and its opposite with equal persuasiveness.

★

BOTH POETS WERE connected for most of their friendship to
another symbolic realm of poetry and ritual—an offshoot of the
Knights Templar, the secret society of poets and financiers. The
Knights were bankers to kings and popes, and issued loans
to build cathedrals and hospitals. They considered themselves
"guardians of the supreme center"; their spiritual authority and
temporal power presumably appealed to both men, who entered
a secret society of their own, the Fedeli d'Amore, the brotherhood of the faithful in love. The Templars had to develop an inner
consciousness of doctrinal unity, blending eastern and western
knowledge. This expansiveness appealed to the poets.

The Fedeli inspired many others: Shelley, Byron and Keats considered themselves a Brotherhood of Love. T. S. Eliot thought of
himself as an Anglican Dante and his mentor, Ezra Pound, an
intellectual Guido. They studied Dante together in their early days
in the British Library. Pound went on to become the great translator of Guido and, like him, a political outcast.

A key meeting place of the Templars is somewhere between
northern Italy and southern France, believed to be Provence. It is
there that the whole hidden geography of Dante's Catharism can
be found. Dante's most moving imagery—the mystic rose of Paradise, the pelican, the white tunics, the three theological virtues of
Faith, Hope and Charity—all are Templar symbols popularized by
this heretical Christian sect named Cathar, from the Greek *kathar-
sis,* meaning purification. Cathars believed things were either
good or evil, and that good required an ascetic renunciation of the
world. Provence was the center for purists who sought to express
their faith best in love. It is also the place where the masters of

the Kabbalah wrote their texts and where Moses de León discovered the Zohar, a manual on the spirit coupling with God.

Provence has disappeared behind Van Gogh's great canvases in sunflowers and heavy brush strokes. Behind them lies a vanished civilization of deep ecstasy known to the troubadour poets, "who had lost the names of the gods and remembered the names of lovers," Pound said. If the troubadours did not invent love itself, they invented the language for it. They were the first to speak of love between two people. "I love you" was an original statement in the eleventh century. "Love" was not a word in Adam or Eve's vocabulary. "We wanted mercy and you gave us knowledge," the children of Adam said to God.

The Fedeli, building on these traditions, created a cult stricter or more subtle than that of the celibate ascetics of the Middle Ages. They called for the purgation of the soul by a refinement of and lordship over the senses. They knew something largely forgotten, that the troubadours were not simply love lyricists; they were lawyers and doctors and counselors to kings engaged in a profound staging of sentiment, intent on putting the largest number of ideas into the fewest lines and thereby shocking people with light, like looking into the sun. For a time the Fedeli's troubadour roots—a sheer love of beauty and a delight in the perception of it—replaced all heavier emotion, but eventually despair, faith, even survival, dominated their circle.

The Templars and troubadours ended badly. The troubadours suffered near genocide in the Albigensian Crusade, begun in 1208 when Pope Innocent III ordered the mystic heretics exterminated and the soul of Europe returned fully to the church. The crusade did not end until 1213. The troubadours' brother knights, the

Templars, would be tortured into admitting they had spit on the cross. Dante vouches for their innocence in the *Comedy*, and he too will be brought up on allegations of magic and witchcraft.

★

GUIDO SHOWS UP in *Inferno* only by allusion. Dante does not even award him the status of one of the noble dead who puts in an appearance. By the time Dante reaches the circle in Hell where he encounters Guido's father, he and Virgil have already been through Limbo, the first circle, where the poets and others who lived before there was a true knowledge of love reside, Virgil among them. They will have gone through the second circle, where lovers whose love wasn't pure and "for the good of the intellect" receive in Hell what they most desired on earth—storms of passion that whirl them around in a ceaseless and joyless act of lovemaking. Since Hell is eternal, they never rest. They will meet the gluttons, the cheapskates, the wasters, the wrathful and the depressed or sullen, then the heretics who inhabit Limbo on down to the sixth circle in Canto 10 (lines 52–69) of *Inferno*, when Dante, led by Virgil, encounters the soul of Guido Cavalcanti's father.

> *Allor surse a la vista scoperchiata*
> *un' ombra, lungo questa, infino al mento:*
> *credo che s'era in ginocchie levata.*
>
> *Dintorno mi guardò, come talento*
> *avesse di veder s'altri era meco;*
> *e poi che'l sospecciar fu tutto spento,*

piagendo disse: "Se per questo cieco
   carcere vai per altezza d'ingegno,
   mio figlio ov'è? e perché non è teco?"

E io a lui: "Da me stesso non vegno:
   colui, ch' attende là, per qui mi mena,
   forse cui Guido vostro ebbe a disdegno."

. . .

Di sùbito drizzato gridò: "Come?
   discesti 'elli ebbe'? non viv' elli ancora?
   non fiere li occhi suio lo dolce lume?"

. . . there rose a shadow, visible
   to the chin; it had raised itself, I think, upon
   its knees.

. . . it said, weeping, "If through this blind prison
   you go by height of genius, where is my
   son and why is he not with you?"

And I to him: "I do not come here alone: he, that awaits
   leads me through this place;
   he whom your Guido held in disdain."

. . . He cried: . . . "Lives he not still? Does not
   the sweet light strike his eyes?"

                    (trans. Wicksteed)

Cavalcanti's father hopes to see his son with Dante. He utters
words that recall God's words to Cain: "My son, where is my

son?": "Where is your brother?" God asks Adam's murderous son. Cavalcanti infers from Dante that Guido—whose love of life on earth, whose belief in individual greatness, led him to achieve his own greatness—no longer feasts "on the sweet light." Devastated, the elder Cavalcanti collapses back into his crypt, among those Dante brands heretics because they believed that pleasure is the highest human good, which meant one needed no gods.

Dante will give Farinata, Guido's father-in-law who raises himself from the same tomb, this message: tell the old man that his son still lives. But it is not true.

Is Dante lying because in Guido's death he suffered the loss of a friend and the loss of innocence? The heresy of the sixth circle is a sin that resides in the mind. Insofar as Dante is concerned, heresy and pleasure are one and the same: an intellectual obfuscation. Guido's father asks a question; he believes by Dante's silence that he hears the answer. Dante tries to speak, but only a partial confession comes from him. In the language he has learned, in the poet he is at this point in his journey, he cannot make himself understood. A new language is needed, one that will carry the truth in all its clarity. No natural philosopher would have said that the mind could sin. Aristotle would not have acknowledged heresy or hypocrisy. These are Dante's demons.

But he is not Dante anymore. He is Dante and Cavalcanti, Dante and Moses in the desert. Experience extends beyond the boundaries of autobiography to become a larger element: Dante discovers the forcefulness of allegory, where his wanderings become a new "exodus." He is all men who have sought freedom and the full expression of the feelings that lie within.

There is a new teacher waiting for him—Beatrice, no longer alive, no longer dead, but in some other state. From here on, love poetry and philosophy would be mingled with sciences like sacred geometry, astrology, light, biology and angelology.

Even Pound will eventually bury Guido's hope of an earthly paradise as the human goal—and a hero that searches for the visible. He wrote a requiem to Guido's idea of love:

I have tried to write Paradise
Do not move
     Let the wind speak
          that is paradise.
Let the Gods forgive what I
        have made.
Let those I love try to forgive
        what I have made.

*

BELOW CAVALCANTI SENIOR lies Lower Hell. Dante and Virgil leave the dead who suffer the excesses of the body—forms of incontinence to Dante. Over the edge of the pit they go, to new depths of misconstrued love: the political evils of fraud and malice. They scare off the Minotaur, the bull more beast than human, who guards the souls in the foulest part of death against any chance of escape. Dante must come as close to death as a living person can to feel the fear, so that life can then have new meaning.

Dantean Pilgrimages

The ruthless and brilliant Lorenzo de' Medici, fifteenth-century prince, patron of Michelangelo and Leonardo, had one lifelong tutor, and he was not the usual whisperer to the throne—neither an assassin nor a banker. He was Marsilio Ficino, Dantista (and Platonist). Renaissance princes did not particularly favor the work of the Middle Ages. In churches, for example: medieval architects envied the spider its web, while Renaissance architects copied the massiveness of mountains. Nor would Dante's message by itself have particularly gratified the Medici prince. Lorenzo had read in Dante that one could pass "Between the wall of earth and the torments" (*Inferno* 10.2), but did *he* have to? Il Magnifico had only to look out of his bedroom window at the Palazzo Vecchio, beautifully cut into the city center, yet not a perfect square. The rulers of Florence wanted to make sure that no stone would ever stand on ground owned by a Farinata—a partisan in the war of Guelfs versus Ghibellines—and so they cut the square short, denying perfection.

Perhaps because he suffered from depression, Lorenzo took these errors personally. They unnerved him. He hungered for the best poetry, pictures, sculpture, a wine that never grew in the belly of a grape. These weren't distractions from statecraft, he advised his court; they *were* statecraft, the chance to make Florence the center of the world. The laws of a state cannot be altered, he said, without altering those also of the Muses.

Leaders and poets make strange bedfellows. Frederick II, king of Sicily from 1198 until 1250, longed to know how God sat on His throne so he could copy the image. He kept poets in his court to advise him on their imaginings of this scene. The surprising part of Lorenzo's story is that he, a student of perfection as a form of power, was drawn to the poet Guido Cavalcanti, the moon to Dante's sun. The Medici prince and his counselor Ficino rhymed their lessons in the meter of Cavalcanti's verse. Lorenzo did not want to think about Cavalcanti; he wanted to think like him. Dante had created a masterwork; but Guido, some believe, had created Dante. The godlike quality of this must have excited Lorenzo.

Is it more godlike to create an artist than a work of art? Perhaps Cavalcanti had found another, sweeter route to Paradise and spared himself the mistakes that sent Dante twisting through Hell, Purgatory and then finally into Paradise. But the deformed palazzo must have suggested otherwise, even for a Medici.

CHAPTER 5

The Golden Sperm

EVERY MORNING BEFORE DAWN, THOMAS AQUINAS'S STU-dents entered their brilliant master's bedchamber to help him rise. They would hoist him from the pallet on which he had passed the night. Thomas thanked God for never letting him forget a word he'd read, and perhaps the same metabolism guaranteed he never lost a calorie he'd consumed. The students carried the master to his desk. From there, Aquinas would enter a palace, built and constructed of mind and soul, of windows and statuary. He had furnished this palace with ideas on ethics, history, God, beauty and the laws of nature. Thomas could sit at his desk and perceive with his eyes everything that is otherwise obscured in the depths of the mind: ideas that often vanish or get hidden over by other things. Writing his *Summa Theologica*—his summing up of all knowledge to his time—was thus not a matter of retrieving files or footnotes. It was not even a matter of thinking. It was all there before him. He did not have to create; he merely had to describe what he saw, relying on Aristotle, whom he called, simply, the Philosopher.

The Thomist method was to think up orders of images with inscriptions on them, memorized in the order of a carefully articulated argument. This technique bears a basic resemblance to the matter of "where did I put my keys?"—except that Thomas was looking for the keys to the universe. The art of memory as the high medievals practiced it allowed them to see everything at once, and to construct intricate works that looked simple—simple because the words were based on images and because all the riches of detail were neatly ordered. When we ask what made Dante Dante, we must peer into how he made use of the storehouse of this saint, before he turned away from this great influencer.

The whole of the Middle Ages is imprinted with the fingerprints of these memory palaces. "The terrifying gargoyles of the cathedral at Chartres and the monstrous designs unfurling on manuscript pages like the Book of Kells are often considered evidence for the tortured psychology of medievals. In fact, these might just be examples of men following classical rules of medieval memory arts," writes the esteemed historian Frances Yates. The grotesque and emotional were created as signs to startle and remind observers that sin and assorted other mistakes deformed one's soul and dwarfed one's future.

Everything from Gothic cathedrals to Byzantine miniatures, Carlovingian ivories and Romanesque capitals tried to be an encyclopedic memory palace of images, clothing a complex thought in great detail and intended to teach a populace that could not read and further persuade those who could. The aim was to be rich, full and complete; not to steal Heaven's fire like the Greek Prometheus, but to enhance the gifts of Paradise. The test of a work of human art was: May I give back to God what God has given me? When a modern-day tourist in Tuscany bites into a ripened tomato or imbibes the grapes, he is taking in this spirit. Agriculture, whose methods date from the same cultural time, shares that ambition. Complexity, which modern Italians battle as much as they cherish it, and which gave us the schemer Machiavelli, is responsible for the riches that define the term "human" at its most ambitious.

Dante was nine when Aquinas died, and the medium of memory is one every Florentine schoolchild would have learned in classes on rhetoric, and as they advanced, from Thomas's commentary *De Memoria et Reminiscentia*. Milk, Thomas writes, perhaps caught in a moment of desire for the gift of Tuscan cows, is a memory palace. If we think of milk, we think of sweetness and the fire of digestion. We think of whiteness, which leads to light and lucidity, which causes whiteness; clarity leads then to air in which light travels, then to moisture, contained in air, then to autumn. For each of these stages, one can attach knowledge about production, the habits of nature, the desires of soul and body, the aims of the deity, the energy of the universe and so on. To recall these ideas, one need only to evoke the taste of the sweet milk. Taste, emotion, become the structure on which to hang many memories and many rules and ideas. The virtue of building a palace such as this one, dedicated to milk, is that one can wander the intricacy of its rooms and see all the ideas. But more than that, one can see them whole as they relate to each other. The order gave rise to a new level of insight: meaning, and the realization that what has happened will happen again; that the whole is contained in its part. Memory = vision = genius.

Dante used that technique to produce his masterpiece. Between his fits of utter worthlessness alternating with exaltations of self-esteem, Dante had to have imagined a sustained work over nearly twenty years. The sheer scale and intricacy of the *Comedy* suggest this. The work is composed of 14,233 deliberately measured verses, built into 100 cantos, each calibrated to a precise rhythm and exhibiting a philosophy that began with Plato and ended with Dante and God and trots across the stage a huge cast of characters. Not outlined or drafted, but imagined slowly and painstakingly, until the edifice was built in his mind and ready to be put to paper. "Dante raised his invisible cathedral," wrote the architectural historian Émile Mâle. "With St. Thomas he was the great architect of the thirteenth century."

He kept his vision alive over nineteen years of trials to make the *Comedy* seem as if it were all one line, the work of one awful moment of birth in which time stopped for genius. Such is the completeness that when we are inside it we lose ourselves. He worked his "sublime geometry" into the fabric of the poem using a very particular form of architecture—the church architect's holy number three. Every medieval church is an entryway or narthex, a main basilica, and an apse with altar—a trilogy that grew for Dante into nine circles of Hell, nine terraces of Purgatory, nine heavens of Paradise. Every character, every idea in the *Comedy*, has a place. This universe is a church that is as rich as a palace.

"The most ardent imagination known in literature was also the most submissive," wrote Mâle. Dante obeyed the laws of medieval architecture, which reflected the rules of divine rhythm found in the universe. But while conforming to the builder's code, he was "seized with a sacred awe from which sprang" a marvel of creativity.

It is tempting to imagine Dante's pockets full of scraps of words which he painstakingly wove together. But this seems unlikely. First because not one word of the *Comedy* survives in

Dante's own handwriting. But also because there is no start and stop in the *Comedy*. The end throws the reader right back to the beginning. The work is as seamless as a living creature born of long gestation—not a Golem stitched together of spare parts.

★

PEOPLE WHO HAVE been to Rome or Tuscany say they have left their souls there. Rome itself is a memory palace: the past as neatly tacked onto the present. Dante, who had been cast out of both places, like his tourist-readers who must also eventually leave, could go back through memory not just to the city of art and the city of empire, but to the entire Roman past, present and future, simply by looking.

Perhaps the cities and works of man that call most to us are those whose scale makes us feel like kings in a larger palace of emperors and gods. Perhaps too the memory palace relieved Dante's homelessness and, in a more existential way, relieves ours too.

★

THE EVIDENCE THAT Dante designed such a palace appears in Canto 3 of *Inferno*. A fantasy castle, whole and integrated with truth, might be the only structure to survive Florence's intense civil strife. Dante had written *Inferno* 1 and 2 while still in Florence—so many scholars believe—plying his usual routine, using pen and paper, presumably. These two poems were found in written form though the pages have since been lost. Cantos 1 and 2 indicate that he set out to write the whole *Comedy* as one book, in which a character goes to Hell, Purgatory and Paradise in a single volume, not a trilogy.

The greatness of Dante comes later, with exile, when he begins Canto 3. We are no longer in a poem—we are in a place. Canto 3 is remarkable in its simplicity and profundity. It contains the most familiar line in all of literature:

LASCIATE OGNI SPERANZA, VOI CH' ENTRATE . . .

ABANDON HOPE, ALL YOU WHO ENTER HERE.

(line 9; trans. Wicksteed)

The text appears as though God wrote in Dante's rhyme scheme. The reader follows him and Virgil past the words on the gate of Hell:

"PER ME SI VA NELLA CITTÀ DOLENTE;
PER ME SI VA NE L'ETERNO DOLORE;
PER ME SI VA TRA LA PERDUTA GENTE."

"THROUGH ME IS THE WAY INTO THE DOLEFUL CITY
THROUGH ME THE WAY INTO THE ETERNAL PAIN;
THROUGH ME THE WAY AMONG THE PEOPLE LOST."

(3.1–3; trans. Wicksteed)

No more little love poems. Dante Alighieri has begun to work on a grand scale. He won't just write about love as romance, but about love as the most important quality of the intellect and therefore the "Archimedean," or pivotal, point of history and creativity. He will make a reader feel everything. He will imagine eyelids as "the lips of the eye," so that feelings, and sufferings, cross the sense barriers (*Inferno* 32.46–47).

As he makes the leap, ending his cowardice, he sees the last image of the living dead—cool, neutral and untouched by love. Virgil tells him, in lines T. S. Eliot will copy in "The Waste Land":

> *"Questi non hanno speranza di morte,*
> *e la lor cieca vita è tanto bassa,*
> *che 'nvidiosi son d'ogne altra sorte.*
>
> *Fama di loro il mondo esser non lassa;*
> *misericordia e giustizia li sdegna:*
> *non ragioniam di lor, ma guarda e passa."*

> ". . . These have no hope of death; and their blind
> life is so mean, that they are envious of every
> other lot.
>
> Report of them the world permits not to exist;
> Mercy and Justice disdains them: let us
> not speak of them; but look, and pass."
>
> (3.46–51; trans. Wicksteed):

Dante tells us these people with no souls are following a flag, a banner:

> *e dietro le venìa sì lunga tratta*
> *di gente, ch'i' non averei mai creduto,*
> *che morte tanta n'avesse disfatta.*

And behind it came a long train of people,
   that I should never have believed death had
   undone so many.

           (3.55–57; trans. Wicksteed)

Dante is among them. In that moment, both he and the reader know what it is to be soulless: "lukewarm." These "neutral angels" whom he describes commit to nothing and envy those who do. Paradise chased them out to keep its beauty intact. Hell doesn't want them either, for "the damned would consider themselves better" than these souls who lived only for themselves: "wretched ones, who were never alive," eager for any place that would take them, even the buried chamber Dante is about to enter as he and Virgil cross "the livid marsh" of the River Acheron into the first circle where the dead souls are arranged in order of the mistakes they made in love. Dante's gulag is as ordered as the biology of the universe.

With this canto, we too are in Dante's capacious memory palace, looking from his mind at his world. Centuries of philosophy are compressed in a few lines of emotionally cathartic poetry. The memory palace is inside Dante. But he is also inside it. We feel, as a reader, like an ant walking a Moebius strip where inside and outside meet on the same plane. We are in Dante's world as thoroughly as he was in God's.

★

THOUGH WE LIVE in a literate culture that has made memory palaces obsolete, one can see that modern works miss something of the respect for wholes and the scope of sacred genius. Modern works are deconstructed—the parts more significant than the whole. Medieval genius is highly constructed. The systems we consider modern—banking, negotiation, faith, individuality—issued from these expansive minds.

The Greeks believed that memory was a mystic faculty, a gift of the gods. One could not sustain the delights of the stomach or be as thoroughly bewitched by the sex organs as by memory. One could use memory to retrieve the lost and reconnect with the dead. Even more astoundingly, one could lose oneself in these images. Medievals favored constructing such palaces out of memory because they wanted to contain within themselves all of God's creation, the good and the bad, the brute and gentle, ordered and visible. It enlarged their minds. "Solemn and rare memory palaces are the most moving," Cicero had written. Often the palaces took the form of churches. If those impossible cathedrals could be built on land, they could surely be built in the mind. It was a sacred obligation to build them: people had a memory of perfection, it was believed, from way back in Eden. This could be aroused through artificial means, like building churches or palaces in the mind filled with images. Memory was wisdom.

To come close to the human-divine boundary—which is protected by certain habits of thought—reason, memory and order must be mastered. One has to become a mirror of God's habit of working. The first work of God is to organize space. For the medievals, this was a reaction to the turbulence of the times: "a place for everything and everything in its place," said the English writer C. S. Lewis. The effect on the reader of Dante is to assume that everything in the *Comedy* has a rightful place, that there are laws of the universe which Dante is offering. If nothing is there by accident or trial, then our job is to figure out the reason. Doing so extends the reader's own range of memory and conditions one to notice the nature of order.

Saint Augustine declared memory "the belly of the soul." All knowledge comes from sense impressions, he wrote, but thinking doesn't work on these in the raw. Images facilitate the making of ideas. Thinking works on images. "The soul never thinks without a mental picture," Aristotle wrote in *De Anima*.

As a schoolboy in the 1270s, Dante would have learned of Augustine's and Aquinas's (Aristotelian) work on memory but had also heard tales of the poet Simonides. At a banquet in ancient Thessaly, Simonides chanted a poem in honor of his host, Scopas, who meanly told him that he would pay him only half the fee agreed upon because Simonides had included a brief tribute to the gods Castor and Pollux. Simonides waited for his diminished pay while the banquet continued. Soon, a message was brought to the poet that two young men were waiting outside for him, and while he was out looking for them, the roof of the banquet hall fell in, crushing all the guests to death. The corpses were so mangled that the relatives could not identify them. But the poet remembered where everyone sat and helped the relatives find their dead. The two young men turned out to be Castor and Pollux. They had paid their share for his song, calling the poet away just before disaster.

Did Dante imagine himself a new Simonides, recounting the dead at their stations in Hell?

★

BY 1303 OR '04, Dante, homeless, his possessions scattered, is developing *Inferno* but is also politically active. He leaves Verona, spurred by an effort to pacify Florence by reuniting the divided Guelfs. In May, he arrives in Arezzo; on July 7, Pope Benedict XI dies suddenly. By July 20, another disaster ensues for the White-Ghibelline alliance, the hodge-podge band of exiles who were routed by Boniface. Dante, having broken with the alliance, is still in Arezzo on the day of Petrarch's birth—Petrarch, who will make every effort to unseat him as the greatest Italian poet. Life seems to be teeming everywhere but under the black cloud that has attached itself to him. Giotto has won the coveted commission to create his frescoes in the Arena Chapel in Padua, and Dante will visit him and watch his friend work. He stays for a while at Treviso, at the court of Gherardo da Camino; and at Venice. A new pope, Clement V, is named on June 5.

Dante is in the eye of the storm. Everywhere, there is unrest if not horrendous violence. Hatred is building against the magicians who still dare to call themselves that. In 1307, on October 13, the Knights Templar, including the Grand Master Jacques du Molay, are arrested all across France; Bernard Gui is quickly rising up the church hierarchy. He will become inquisitor at Toulouse. Minor kings spark hopes of empire—hence peace—only to fail. On July 7, King Edward I of England dies of dysentery in Cumbria on his way to invade Scotland. Lack of stable leadership is the bane of western Europe in these years: the world is going to Hell. Inspiration for the *Inferno* is not lacking.

Hell becomes a realized world. Dante fills it with real and imagined Florentines. The structure, like a funnel, narrows at its bottom and core to the throne of Satan. From there, a sphincter leads out to the entry to Purgatory. Hell is Italians, Purgatory is a church of souls and, true to form, the style of *Purgatorio* is the sermon. Paradise will be the apse, the transforming altar. So rises Dante's imagined church.

Each place Dante goes in this vision-palace, his church, he might well imagine the leaders there falling in love with him and bestowing on him a part in their rule. When he leaves this palace for "real life" of the open road and political catastrophe he does not lose this divinity of mind. Dante could look through the forest, which human sight cannot do itself. He could see a slope leading out onto a high hill, and from there he could see the whole of his life and its meaning. The wood was his inferior world; the slope, his improvement; and the hill—Paradiso—his perfection. In order to understand the things of the lower world, he has only to look from on high, and thus attain a more certain knowledge of inferior things.

*

"SELDOM, VERY SELDOM, he shows us his writing tools," poet Osip Mandelstam wrote. "A pen is called *penna,* that is, it participates in a bird's flight; ink is *inchiostro,* that is, belonging to a cloister." Monks create cheap ink from insect larvae plucked from the maples in their gardens. Reduce the placental sacs to dust. Mix with rainwater and white wine. Soak until ready to add to a bath of sulfuric acid poured over nails.

Lines of verse from this concoction are also called *inchiostri,* after the ink; lines are the substance of this bitter, heady infusion. The atmosphere of writing tools is useful, because Dante never forgets the origin of things. The pen is connected to flight:

E come augelli surti di rivera,
  quasi congratulando a lor pasture,
  fanno di sé or tonda or altra schiera,

sì dentro ai lumi sante creature
  volitando cantavano, e faciensi
  or D, or I, or L in sue figure.

Like birds which, risen from the bank
  as if rejoicing at their pasture,
  make themselves now into a rounded, now into an
    elongated flock,

so within lights the holy creatures,
  flying, sang, and made themselves
  now into a D, now into an I, now into an L in their
    configurations.

(*Paradiso* 18.73–78; trans. Mandelstam)

"Books fly!"—"*Libri volant!*"—Bernard warned when imagining the dangerously free passage of Abelard's treatises questioning church practice. Dante wrote during a technological revolution when books were becoming smaller, lighter and even faster to circulate. Books could be carried and held; they did not require special furniture to rest upon for reading. The thousands of students who flocked to school in Paris and Bologna craved a continuing supply of secular literature and now could read books at home or in daylight, free of the hallucinatory sputter of a monastery candle. When Dante completed *Inferno*, it was copied onto paper with the other works of the vulgar, or vernacular, language—and spread quickly. Yet Dante fancied the *Comedy* being read by a reader at a desk, as he says in *Paradiso* 10.22, off a stately large parchment. That is not what he got. The first manuscripts of the *Comedy* are believed to have been roughly ten inches tall, not the large quarto sheets worked over by nuns and monks drawing in the dying and deformed Gothic but copied into cursive script called *bastarde*! It was not what he wanted.

Schooled at Santa Maria Novella in Florence, Dante would have pored over texts the size of newspaper pages like the *New York Times*'s. When one turned the pages, a sound like thunder issued from the huge heavy sheets. They begged to be turned, like bottles of wine. Parchment was made of animal skins, dried and then softened; touch kept them supple for a thousand years. The words were considered holy, and the scribes who lettered them were in God's service. For every correct word they committed to the skins, a sin or mistake was expunged. Write a word, have your past edited: it seemed like a better-than-fair trade. Scribes were housed in fortresses, usually downstairs. Though it was drafty and sunlight was scarce, it meant they were safe from arrows and flying dung.

To put "pen to paper" in this culture was still a sacred act. Scribes believed they were writing God's word when they wrote in Latin. The world is itself a book. Scholars say the Middle Ages were the time of great "textuality." Everything worth anything got described as a book. A tree was a word that symbolized the Tree of Life, just as people wore flesh over souls. The church called Jesus *Logos,* the Word. John the Evangelist, Jesus' apostle, wrote, "And I went to the angel, saying unto him that he should give me the book. And he said to me: Take the book and eat it up. . . . And I took the book from the hand of the angel and ate it up; and it was in my mouth, sweet as honey; and when I had eaten it my belly was bitter" (*Apocalypse* of John, 10:9–10). Increasingly, however, works like the *Comedy* were copied by students and priests needing extra income and by women working at home, who would carry their finished pages to binders.

From inside his memory palace/church, Dante tells us he is a scribe, a copyist, a translator.

> *I' mi son un che, quando*
> *Amor mi spira, noto, e a quel modo*
> *ch'e'ditta dentro vo significando.*

> I am one who, when
> Love breathes in me, takes note, and as it is
> dictated within, go setting it down.

> (*Purgatorio* 24.52–54; trans. Merwin)

The dictator, he calls God: the taskmaster, the real poet, not the so-called poet he considers himself. He calls himself a scribe. The whole work exists. Dante is simply reading it, taking it down as dictation.

Dante is a copyist bent over nearly double "who squints in fright at the illuminated original lent to him from the prior's library." Most of the books making their way out of the monastic library were illustrated, for nonreaders, but for persuasive purposes too. An Irish codex of the twelfth century suggests the connection between word and image: "What this picture allows you to grasp with the bodily senses is that which you should bring forth spiritually."

"I will labor a little more," Mandelstam imagines Dante saying, "and then I must show my notebook, drenched with the tears of a bearded schoolboy, to a most strict Beatrice, who radiates not only glory but literacy too." When Dante shows her his work in Purgatory's last terrace, a plain in the earthly paradise, she tells him they are foolish and uninformed compared to what she will show him.

When Dante does write, chances are that he writes on paper, not costly parchment or vellum. Tuscan paper in the years before paper mills was brewed of old undergarments, animal parts and hemp, boiled in the paper-maker's cauldron. The market in spare parchment is monopolized by the chief enemy of books in the Middle Ages: perfumers—biblioclasts, book destroyers, who routinely burned papyrus to give forth a pleasing aroma.

★

IT WILL TAKE another 150 years for the inventor of the printing press Johannes Gutenberg to say, "With twenty-six soldiers I have conquered the world." In the interim, books were few; many were lost. And what of Dante's own books?

His richest hosts would have had considerable libraries. Francesca da Rimini, the eternal lover in *Inferno* 5, was an incorrigible reader of romances. Books were plentiful. No one knows how many books Dante had at his disposal in the years of composing *Inferno*. He seems to have read everything, from classical texts, collections of Provençal poets, Italian poets and church fathers' works to treatises on medicine, astrology and geography. He could have gotten them on trips to Bologna and to Paris, eventually—the book capitals of the thirteenth and fourteenth centuries. Maybe he memorized some of them, as the

Greeks had memorized their texts. A large part of his education in exile would have come not only from reading but from hearing. Sermons and lectures were ubiquitous, and there was always a discussion in which to participate.

*

WORDS HELD IN the mind, built into images to be inhabited: this is what alchemists too were looking for: the transformative agent, the "golden sperm"—as alchemy's etymology is believed to be. Words can change lives. But not just any word or words. The grail of language would be revealed, Dante believed, in a cleaner, clearer sound.

"I have wandered through almost every place where our language is spoken, like a beggar displaying the wounds of fate. . . ." Dante writes between 1304 and 1307 (*Il Convivio*). When does it dawn on him that he is condemned by the very language he loves? The Italian language rose before him like the walls of the cities, meant to keep out the unwanted. The dozens of dialects mark a stranger. They carry out Florence's unjust sentence of exile. Writers think the whole world is their native land, but a poor wanderer such as Dante was lost everywhere. Walking from town to town, Dante could barely make himself understood. The dialects were fiercely different, sometimes from city to city, sometimes from neighborhood to neighborhood. Everyone is exiled, Dante believes. It is a human condition; no one can talk to anyone else. If there is no universal justice, a poet must create a language by which everyone could understand each other. Dante conceived his mission as finding one unifying language of love and empire to fill the vacuum left by failed leaders and empty courts of justice. In

1305, he writes in *De Vulgari Eloquentia* (On Vernacular Eloquence) of his search for a common tongue that will be a "poetic ethics." It must be a language so basic that it will be understood by all and would, in effect, negate the sentence against him. If he could speak and be understood throughout Italy, no door would be closed to him. Everyplace would be home. By 1303, '04, or '05, with the new beginning of *Inferno* and Canto 3, he embarks on this new course, creating a new language.

Dante's impulse is to go further than Aquinas—to set his own "Summa" into poetry, the language of the emotions. "Put bits into horses' mouths and one can control their bodies. So with the tongue: a small member but capable of a huge blaze," Dante would write around this time in *Il Convivio,* which means The Banquet. He named this work in homage to Plato's *Symposium,* which means "drinking party" and is often translated as "feast." Dante lays out a critique of his own love poems and a general recipe for knowledge. It is incomplete, but certain of one point: Words represent fire, keeping the wheel of existence white-hot. No one can subdue the tongue, especially when it is used to praise and curse as Dante is busy doing in the *Comedy.*

But where could one find the makings of a universal language in which to cast this work? Latin was the universal language of the educated, the tongue of theologians and lawyers and the patriarchy—the elements of malign authority. But Dante was looking for a common language, and the most common would be one of emotion. For that, Italian, not Latin or logic, was best. But which Italian?

Dante's tendency is to look always for first principles. Where had things gone wrong first? Babel Tower was where the problem began. Masons, bricklayers, quarriers and artists were building a tower to heaven, a monstrously brilliant creation. That these workers had gotten so far with their project was the result of the one shared language. But God, angry at this pride-driven assault on his kingdom, changed their unified language to many languages, throwing their efforts into confusion. Dante knew that the many languages eventually spread throughout Europe and became French, German, Spanish, Greek and Asian languages. The worst part of God's vengeance was not the workers' inability to speak to each other, but the rupture of that unifying language which man shared with God.

One language after Babel seemed linked to the cosmos: Hebrew. Adam, who did not have an infancy, therefore had spoken a perfect language with God. (*Infans* is Latin for "being unable to speak.") But Hebrew too was corrupted, the result of Adam's fall. Dante's favorite poems were the psalms of the Jewish King David, poems also of exile, war and love. Dante sensed that they held a magic beyond the dark smudges of words on the page. Such words had changed the lives of their original listeners, inspiring valiant acts in war, strength to cleanse the soul, and the unity to build a nation. But now the psalms were only the shadow of a shadow, verse translated from Hebrew into Greek, a language lost in the Middle Ages, and then into Latin. What happened to the psalms happened in every act of communication. People were using words that were increasingly distant from the language Adam spoke, the pure language of Paradise. Dialects created narrowness, bias and confusion.

What could work? Dante considered all the dialects he heard, especially his own, the burlesqueries of Tuscan dialects. Who wanted to hear poetry from the same mouths that brayed "Let's eat" or "The boys are marching from Pisa to Florence"? That was *vulgar* vulgar, not illustrious vulgar. The illustrious vulgar: "illustrious" means "shining with light"; "vulgar" means "vernacular, or common, shared, expressive language."

Maurice Maeterlinck, a nineteenth-century theorist of language, said, "I am disposed to believe that every language always thinks more than the man, even the man of genius, who employs it, and who is only its heart for the time being." Dante was very aware of his language's political and personal impact. *Dolce stil nuovo* was a new style he loved in his courtship years in Florence. Borrowed from the troubadours, it sweetened love's miseries. But this language wasn't deep or broad enough for those he now wanted to hear him. He wanted to be read by people who did not know Latin: merchants, artisans, shopkeepers, artists, accountants and the majority of women. In Italian cities, as early as the fourteenth century, many people of all classes were able to read and write. Ten years after Dante's death, registers show that in Florence nearly 60 percent of children ages six to thirteen attended school.

Increasingly the common language was the language of commerce, which seemed to know no boundaries. But merchants skimp on the truth. Courtly dialects are the early version of a business *lingua franca*. The Sicilian dialect—slow and soft—once a medium for distinguished poets and illustrious courtiers, had become tainted by fraud and avarice. Dante notes that Italians have unifying gestures, fashions and beliefs. Within this common behavior a language is certainly concealed: a universal Italian language (*De Vulgari Eloquentia* 30). He is dreaming now for sure, but not irrationally. Just as radio and later television newscasters drummed a standard dialect into American ears in the early twentieth century, neither Boston Brahmin nor Brooklynese, Dante wanted to create a "cardinal, courtly, and curial vernacular" which belongs to all the towns of Italy but which does not belong to any of them" (*De Vulgari Eloquentia* 1). This is the penultimate task: to invent this language and restore a ladder to the heavens.

Dante compares his task of creating a new language to a search for "the panther whose fragrance hovers everywhere, tantalizing beyond entrapment." He imagines he is hunting it from city to city, to capture it for his memory palace, to infuse its hypnotic scent into his poem.

From Aristotle to the bestiaries of Byzantium, the panther is not hunted, but hunts. "The man who confronts it must be of like valor." Like the fox and other cunning creatures, "it possesses the quality of prudence, and an intelligence that proceeds by subterfuge and knows how to conceal its aims. But the panther's deceit is more subtle than the fox's: it has recourse to odor. In fact, the panther is a perfumed beast, which also distinguishes it from all other animals. No creature naturally emits a good smell, writes Theophrastus, except for the panther. Aristotle poses the question, without answering it clearly, as to why the animals all smell bad except for the panther. In the town of Tarsus, there had been a prized perfume called "panther" but its formula had already been lost by the time of Pliny (23–79).

Dante is in a sense no longer wandering. He believes he is following a sublime creature, this panther, toward a new power to spread his ideas. But he does not entirely succeed. The ambition informs the *Comedy,* but as the translator Philip Wicksteed wrote, "The illustrious language which Dante separates from all the local dialects of Italy is mainly based on the speech of Tuscany which he so bitterly derides." Illustrious vernacular or common speech, it will turn out, is not a given language, "but is what causes one language or another to express itself nobly." Short of creating a new language, he creates a quality of expression. Umberto Eco suggests that Dante doesn't find the panther; he *becomes* the panther by speaking and living a universal language of redemption.

Dantean Pilgrimages

By the time of the Renaissance, Italy itself seemed to have become Dante's memory palace. Science was summoned to map his poetic terrain as if it were the contours of earth. Galileo, however, came to conclude that Hell did not exist, a discovery "that got his career started," according to historian of physics Mark Peterson. As a young man, Galileo, a medical school dropout, tutored in mathematics and assisted his father in remarkable experiments on the pitch of plucked strings. With the help of his more illustrious brother Francesco, who had been made a cardinal, Galileo was invited to address the Florentine Academy some time around 1585. He knew that a talk on Dante would be a crowd-pleaser. The Academy had "as one of its chief functions the glorification of [its patrons] the Medici in every intellectual arena." Galileo spoke on the geometry of Dante's *Inferno* and charmed the audience.

The task before Galileo was to prove that the vault that covers Dante's Inferno could support itself and not fall into the hole. By measuring the radius of the earth and the land mass of Jerusalem over which the Inferno is stretched, according to Dante, one arrives at a model that suggests a large domed roof, somewhat smaller than Brunelleschi's famous dome over the Florence Cathedral. Galileo had come up with a proof, and commissions, and support came flowing in to the young Galileo as a result of these lectures.

But this was a mistake, as Galileo must have realized soon after. The problem of scale and strength of materials occupied his thought. From this problem and the realization that he was wrong, Galileo embarked upon studies of the weight of bodies, including "his famous observations on why animals cannot simply be scaled up: their bones must become proportionally thicker as they get larger."

By reflecting on his error, Galileo learned what a geometer can do. "By the use of geometry," says Peterson, "we see beyond the limitations of our senses, reasoning about otherwise inaccessible things. This insight is, in a way, the heart of physics as Galileo came to understand it."

Galileo disowned the lectures. When the Florentines begged for a copy, none was produced. Contemporary historian Peter Pesic contends that the reason was Florentine politics, enmeshed in a culture of attack and counterattack. His work on Dante came to terrify Galileo. By 1609, he knew Dante's Hell was structurally unsound, calling into question whether Dante had really entered Hell near Naples, where another Medici scholar asserted the doorway would be found, through which vast subterranean spaces unfolded, supporting the theory that the domed earth did not fall into the Inferno. Galileo adopted Copernicanism, observing that the sun, not the earth, was the center of the universe. Church opposition to Copernicus was growing. His book would be condemned in 1616, and charges were brought against Galileo in 1633. "In the midst of these dangers," writes Pesic, "Galileo would have had good reason to avoid showing that hell was physically impossible, at least the literal hell of Dante. The status of hell touches moral questions of punishment for sin and also the privilege of popes, as successors of Peter, keepers of the keys of hell no less than heaven."

Dante said that everything in the *Comedy* could be understood allegorically, morally, literally and personally. Whether Hell existed, Galileo came to doubt. Whether Dante had been there, or whether Galileo would see it in his own trials and his brush with the plague, is not easy to question.

CHAPTER 6

The Difficult Discipline of "As Pleased Another"

PERHAPS GALILEO WAS MISTAKEN: THE DOORWAY TO HELL did exist, but it could not be found again until the medieval twentieth century.

Primo Levi, inmate of Auschwitz in 1944 and 1945, was asked by the twenty-four-year-old French *Pikkolo,* or junior guard, of his *Kommando,* to teach him Italian. Levi chose the Ulysses canto, *Inferno* 26, in which the shade of Ulysses tells Dante how he met his death. The occasion for the lesson is the guard Jean's mission to carry the day's soup from kitchen to barracks. Jean has chosen Levi to assist him, a great reward, though the hundred-pound kettle could buckle the knees. The task meant a release from the underground chemical bunker to which they were assigned for a brief walk in the sunshine.

Levi struggles to remember Dante's verses and to translate them into French. His memory falters until he gets to the verse "I put forth on the deep open sea"—"*Ma misi me per l'alto mare aperto*" (line 100). He tries to convey the power of it—*misi me*—a man trying to crash through a barrier. Thinking of the barbed wire around them both, guard and prisoner, Levi says that he and Jean know that feeling well. Ulysses' words of persuasion to his crew, the invitation which Dante, who reveled in the arts of persuasion, delighted in writing, slowly return to Levi. They are words that inspire his crew, now "old and slow," to risk everything for a glimpse of the truth, for one last noble mission:

> '. . . *Considerate la vostra semenza:*
> *fatti non foste a viver come bruti,*
> *ma per seguir virtute e canoscenza.'*

> '. . . Consider your origin:
> you were not made to live like brutes,
> but to follow virtue and knowledge.'

> (118–20)

It sounds like the voice of God. It has called to Dante, and to Ulysses. Jean is moved and Levi struggles to remember more:

> *quando n'apparve una montagna, bruna*
> *per la distanza. . . .*

> when there appeared to us a mountain,
> dim because of distance

> (133–34)

Levi remembers his own mountains near his home in Turin, and almost cries out, "*Pikkolo,* don't let me think of my mountains." He struggles to recall the last four lines that end with Ulysses' shipwreck just as the boat is lifted to the sight of Mount Purgatory—their goal. Three times, Ulysses' boat spins around in the waves, and on the fourth it crashes, the sea closing over him, "as pleased an Other." Levi stops at the words *"com' altrui piacque." Altrui*—"an Other," the word for *God* which cannot be spoken in Hell.

As Levi tries to explain the words to Jean, an intuition of why they are in Auschwitz flashes across his mind. Like Ulysses, the realization comes crashing down on him as the cook announces the day's watery soup: cabbage and turnips. Levi, a Jew, is like Ulysses in Hell, shipwrecked for no reason other than pursuing a noble desire.

*

CANTO 26 IS the favorite of T. S. Eliot, Machiavelli and all those who consider Dante the poet's poet. It is the no-turning-back episode of Dante's journey. The whole of Dante's life is to transform himself from pilgrim or seeker, lost in his own questions, into the poet, certain and transcendent. *Inferno* 26 is the moment Dante compares his ambition to his craft, and he does this by coming face-to-face with Ulysses to look into the mirror of his *own* soul. Dante and Ulysses are in the same boat: two wanderers, they dare all for a certain kind of knowledge. But one drowns and one is saved—depending entirely, it seems, on the pleasure of God, not on one's own dexterity. Dante is about to learn what every reader of this canto longs to know: how to become godlike, or Fortune's favored child.

The answer is in the phrase *com' altrui piacque.* A reader may begin where Levi and Ulysses stopped, with these ominous words. He will see more than the words. Here are the conditions that led the poet to the idea that he expressed in these images. As

Dante's life becomes increasingly introspective, let us follow him as these words take on breadth and depth in his mind.

The most modest of the three words is *come*: "as," or "like." Dante, who compared himself often to the planets, says he is *like* one of the seven wandering stars. He took as meaningful that he was born a Gemini. In his day, astrology was psychology. The whole of life's journey was to slough off the qualities one acquired as one fell through the skies to earth—the Jovian, the venereal, martial, mercurial qualities, etc., that were left by a brush with one of the seven planets. Gemini is the imprint of restlessness symbolized by the twins, so the ancient astrologers believed. The planet marked a person with dual desires: for sorrow and joy, love and war. When a Gemini found love, he longed for war; he was always on the move. Dante must have felt farthest from home at this time in his life, in the years 1306–8. He must have asked himself if his exile proved a point in Florence or Rome. Did it deepen the vision he sought? What was served by his wandering?

These were the years when he passed through small towns the Florentines denigrated, saying that the bread they fed their dogs surpassed that eaten elsewhere. How often did Dante have bread to eat? Were there ever coins in his pocket? One assumes he took dozens of odd jobs during his exile, tutoring or writing letters. If he were lucky enough to get a job sweeping a piazza on the morning of a feast day, he could earn 30 scudi—enough for dinner and a night's lodging.

Come: he is looking for equivalences: What are things really like? What do they share? What makes things different? When he reaches Paradiso, he will not need comparisons anymore. He will see things for what they really are.

"I am a tired swimmer," Dante says at the outset of Dorothy

Sayers's translation. He is not mad enough to "swim" the wide ocean; but he is at sea, at the mercy of his fate.

> *E come quei, che con lena affannata*
> *uscito fuor del pelago a la riva,*
> *si volge a l'acqua perigliosa, e guata:*

> And as he, who with panting breath has escaped
> From the deep sea to the shore, turns to the
> Dangerous water and gazes:

> (*Inferno* 1.22–24; trans. Wicksteed)

Dante uses "as" in his famous phrase not only as an equivalence, but as a pronoun: *that which* pleases an Other. From Ulysses' fate, it is clear that the journey is not the reward. If it were that simple, the search for knowledge would have spared the old man. The journey requires more than will and a destination.

*

THE MIDDLE AGES were full of *"folle voles"*—"mad journeys": knights chasing dragons, crusaders routing infidels, sailors searching for new lands, popes plunging into politics. Patience is for wines and cheeses and siestas. Otherwise, Italy does not hold still. All those in Hell are there because of mad voyages.

In 1291, the attraction of the perilous voyage had reached its apogee. The year the Crusades ended at Acre, Marco Polo was in China packing his bags for home. The tale of his voyage, when it was published at the end of the century, would be a bestseller. In the same year, two galleys were outfitted in splendid fashion by the Genoese. Water, grapes, salt cod, fig pies, salamis of seven kinds, cases of wine—rosé, white and red—olives and oils and two Franciscan friars were loaded aboard. Captain Ugolino Vivaldi sailed for the Straits of Gibraltar. He never made it, but there was no evidence of shipwreck, fueling the belief that Vivaldi had reached the Pillars of Hercules, as the Straits were then called. There lay the secret of eternal life. If that were the case, one would not bother to return, even to Genoa, so rich with wine that the flies got drunk on the surplus. Vivaldi was named the new Ulysses.

There is a medieval fable (based on Homer's *Odyssey* 11) that Ulysses had returned home only to make one last journey. He would travel far into the sea carrying an oar over his shoulder, to a place where people have forgotten the existence of the sea and the use of the oar. There he will plant it in the earth and a new civilization will grow. Vivaldi seemed the fulfillment of this prophecy, and the stories fed Italian wanderlust.

Partly what made the Italians such robust sailors was a heritage that went back to the Etruscans, earlier than the Romans, who were the Mediterranean's most expert pirates and merchants (these callings were one and the same). What the ancient Greeks called Scylla and Charybdis, the whirlpools of death, were likely to be pirate bands of Etruscans who guarded the channel of the Strait of Messina. Aeneas traveled far and founded Italy. Columbus, Vespucci and the Venetian adventurer Casanova wandered afar. And so Italians embark on these *folle voles,* following the roads they could map only by the stars, and inspiring others to follow. Nietzsche, perhaps the unhappiest Dantista, would travel to Genoa because he identified with Columbus. He even persuaded the captain of a Sicilian sailing freighter to let him go along to Messina as the sole passenger. The adventure lasted exactly four days. They came nowhere near a shipwreck. He concluded it is not the sea's calm and serenity that gratify the sailor. Sailors pray for waves, not calm seas. The problem is the "sea of existence" has become calm, and our searches are limited.

Sailing and transgressing: these are companion ideas since ancient times. They suggest ambition is a kind of wandering, and something more: that life can be lived fully only by means of things that can be fatal to it. Shipwreck is such. In a post-Freudian world, we say the destiny we can will into being is not the destiny we want. Dante wanted to meet the fate that was not in his mortal hand, but in the hands of "an Other." But how to reach that further shore without shipwreck, without suffering the failure of "men who abused their genius, perverting it to wiles and stratagems," as poet John Ciardi wrote of Ulysses?

Dante suggests that the soul, like the great sailors, also wanders alone. " 'Issues from the hand of God, the simple soul' / to a flat world of changing lights and noise," T. S. Eliot wrote in "Animula," inspired by *Inferno* 26 to imagine how boring the soul's life is in a world dominated by knowledge and nothing deeper or more mysterious. The soul which is stamped with the poetry of creation longs for more than the world provides. Eliot wrote in homage to the Roman emperor Hadrian's famous farewell to his own dying soul, headed off to the gloomy underworld. No emperor has written anything like it before or since:

Animula vagula blandula
hospes comesque corporis
quae nunc abibis
in loca pallidula rigida nudula
nec ut soles dabis iocos

Poor little, lost little, sweet little soul,
My body's companion and friend,
Where are you going to now, little soul,
Pale little, stiff little, bare little soul,
Now that the jokes have to end?

(trans. Mary Hodgson)

Hadrian saw shipwreck ahead. The end of life seemed to promise no more. But Dante in Hell needs to find out where the imperial soul goes, souls of those who crave to know. Do the jokes have to end?

*

IN *INFERNO* 26, Dante plunges into the circle of liars, thieves and consultants—men who fall in love with their own words or ideas. To use superior wisdom in deceiving others is spiritual theft; and the consultants, who are guilty of that, are running along the chasm, each "stolen" from view, bound in the flame of their own consciousness and tormented by this burning. Dante's eye is caught by an "old world flame," which Virgil recognizes as the shade of Ulysses, murmuring, blown about by the wind. Dante thinks back to Florence's criminal sons and realizes that his ideas of justice for his enemies only helped them deceive him.

The dead in Hell are reduced to their true selves, no flesh to hide their real natures. In medieval art, the soul was often depicted as a naked body. Ulysses burned with mad passions in life, but now in Hell, he simply burns. He is covered in fire, his tongue a flame. Dante notices two things: one, that the torments in Hell don't get worse as the crimes darken. Ulysses trapped in a flame is no worse than the betrayers' weeping tears that freeze into icicles and cut their eyeballs as they weep. They are not worse off than Pier della Vigna, one of the first practitioners of the melliflous sonnet, and a suicide, who is turned into a plant in Hell and communicates only by oozing green sap and hissing through it.

Ulysses, pompous, speaks as a tragic hero would, in hyperbole, shifty and pretentious. "If they can speak within those sparks," Dante says to Virgil (lines 64–69), "Master, I pray you . . ." Translate, he begs Virgil. He does not know Greek. But he is also suggesting he has no truck with Ulysses' high style. He wants to know how Ulysses perished, but Ulysses will speak only to a *famous* poet—it doesn't matter that Virgil has written angrily of the Greeks, of their fraudulence and treachery. Although Dante, perhaps in a swipe at Virgil, is suggesting that Virgil too is a deceiver, trying to pass himself off as the greater poet—Homer—in this dark world. It is Homer who, ages ago, memorialized this corrupt Greek journeyer. Ulysses had deceived his enemies. He created the Trojan Horse, promising gifts of peace and then murdering the Trojans he deceived. He stole Achilles from his mother, who hid her son on an island of women to keep him from the battle she prophesied would kill him.

Ulysses tells Virgil he came back to Penelope, his wife, and to Telemachus, his beloved son, but he could not overcome a hunger to know more. All he wanted was another heroic enterprise. So he gathered his former companions, "old and slow," and convinced them to make one more voyage into the ocean to "the unpeopled world beyond the Sun . . . : you were not made to live like brutes but to pursue virtue and knowledge."

"And having turned our ship to the morning, with our oars we made wings for our mad flight . . ."

What are Ulysses and his men doing rowing across the ocean with oars—as foolish as Sayers's "tired swimmer"? Plato writes in his dialogue *Phaedo* that there are two kinds of navigation: one sails through life by examining the nature of material things; the other way is moving by one's own reason, *with oars*. But reason proves to be arrogance in an ocean of uncertainty. The difficulty is not merely to see the truth, but to arrive at it, and Ulysses and his ship are swallowed up in a storm.

". . . *Noi ci allegrammo, e tosto tornò in pianto;*
  ché da la nova terra un turbo nacque,
  e percosse del legno il primo canto.

Tre volte il fé girar con tutte l'acque;
  a la quarta levar la poppa in suso,
  e la prora ire in giù, com' altrui piacque,
  infin che'l mar fu sovra noi richiuso."

"We joyed, and soon our joy was turned to grief;
  for a tempest rose from the new land, and
  struck the forepart of our ship.

Three times it made her whirl round with all
  the waters; at the fourth, made the poop rise
  up and prow go down, as pleased Another, till
  the sea was closed above us."

(26.136–42; trans. Wicksteed)

Ulysses moved hardened warriors by the power of his speech: his deception ended up becoming self-deception. He believed in promises on which he could not deliver. In seeking everything, he lost everything.

Ulysses' journey is about the journey of the soul. Dante knows that Virgil's own hero, Aeneas, on a similar voyage, had founded Rome. Ulysses too burned with the dream of discovering a new world. Both wanderings might have seemed heroic. Why, then, Dante wonders, is Ulysses prevented from achieving Aeneas's goal? Are the same large ambitions too proud and lofty for him to hope to attain?

*

THESE SAME AMBITIONS inflame those Dantisti who believe with Ulysses. The poet Percy Shelley left London in 1817 for northern Italy to follow Dante's trail in exile for the purpose of educating his soul. He studied the poem, wrote in Dante's *terza rima* style, and walked the sites Dante traveled. Shelley and two friends outfitted a boat to sail from Pisa to Lerici. The last words he wrote in his notebook were: "The Spring rebels not against winter but it succeeds it—the dawn rebels not against night but it disperses it." He had visions, he calls them "visitations," of "the sea . . . flooding the house and it is all coming down." His wife Mary Shelley woke him from the nightmares that also terrified her.

She begs him not to go. But he is caught up in the madness and hires a boat. It is summer, and there are squalls. A storm rises quickly and the waves become "mountains high." A sailor who testified later that he tried to convince the captain of Shelley's boat to come aboard his larger vessel or at least to lower his sails heard a voice—high-pitched and unmistakably Shelley's—call out to stop the captain from lowering the mast. The boat went down under full sail.

Shelley's body floated to shore days later, his arms and face eaten away by fish. Given the devastation, it was burned, like Ulysses', but not before his friend Trelawny removed his heart and kept it for months in a mahogany chest in the British consul's wine cellar.

*

PIACQUE: PAST TENSE of *piacere*, to please: the next important word in Dante's phrase "as pleased Another," the reason Ulysses cites for his shipwreck within sight of his greatest success—the arrival at the glorious mountain of Purgatory. *Piacere* is similar to the words for "calm," "placid," "to be agreeable to God." But what pleases not just others, but an Other—that is, God?

In the Middle Ages, one of the greatest offerings to God was words. Jesus was Logos; man could make a spiritual offering of Logos. "Speech," says a sarcastic divine of the seventeenth century, "was given to the ordinary sort of men to communicate their mind; but to wise men to conceal it." That irony was lost on Florentine schoolmasters who taught that Fortune, the stubborn goddess of fate, could be flattered by speech. Words were potent and their mastery was highly sought, according to Brunetto Latini, the Florentine master of rhetoric, Dante's own teacher, who wrote in his widely used textbook *La Rettorica* "that mad and daring men are those mad and quick to do things which are not to be done." Yet Brunetto told his students that the origin of the political order is found in the "gift of language as the mirror of man's presence."

Brunetto taught his students rhetoric as the basis of the arts and sciences. The *trivium* in medieval education was a "three way" curriculum consisting of rhetoric, grammar and logic. Rhetoric, the art of speech, offered the means to use language persuasively to open up men's souls. There was vast proof that it could do so: Christianity itself was a revolution in rhetoric. Before Christ, one had to adapt one's style to one's subject. Talking to soldiers, one would use the low style, then switch to the high style to address one's superiors. Jesus changed all that by asking the Samaritan women for a glass of water. Humble language could thereafter be used to describe sublime things. Ulysses, employing the high style of tragedy, became a warning to Dante. "Comedy" was the low style, humble, the language of the streets. Virgil had used the high tragic style to write about the hero Aeneas. Then Christianity disrupted this neat division. This is the revolution: the humble speech of sacred scripture.

Dante went further than his teacher Brunetto. His rhetoric was a form of *logology:* a process of putting God into words—that means he made the effort to write a sacred work, as distinct from *theology,* which is putting words to the description of God. Language has the power of weapons. The worst would be to leave them to those whom Saint Augustine calls "the salesmen of words." As Dante hears Beatrice's own words, he finds they are plain and smooth. He knows that language conveys lies as easily as truth. He had been charged with crimes he had not committed. He could not persuade his enemies of the value of justice, harmony and an authority higher than morality, namely aesthetics. Words had failed him.

Dante begins to worry about the limits and excesses of art and the artful mind. Ulysses believes that the distance between truth and lies can be bridged by knowledge. He convinces his companions to make this voyage by seducing them with words. And of course, he convinces himself. It is a kind of thievery, secret and furtive. But far from being the master of his art, Ulysses is possessed by it. Knowledge is not the way to the mind of God, as Adam's dismissal from Eden proved. Knowledge is not Paradise. It is not perfection. It is not bliss. Ulysses mentions all the places he has traveled, from Morocco to Sardinia, Seville and Ceuta, confusing knowledge with wisdom. He has succumbed to the literalness of language, trapped by his own tongue.

Ulysses equates virtue and knowledge. Dante sees that they are not the same thing: to know virtue is not necessarily to have it. Only uncompromising virtue will allow him to make his way back from the loftiest journey ever taken. Dante doesn't want to become like Ulysses. He is afraid of possible treachery in his own artfulness and the madness of his journey.

> . . . ché nessuna mostra 'l furto,
> e ogne fiamma un peccatore invola.

> Not one reveals the theft
>   and every flame steals a sinner.

> (26.41–42; trans. Wicksteed and others)

Rhetoric, Dante sees, is not a pure art. In *Inferno* 5, Dante faints when Paolo and Francesca tell him they committed adultery under the influence of a book they have read. The power of language led two people to believe they were in love and commit a crime. Rhetoric is a tool to manipulate and order historical consciousness. As Brunetto taught, rhetoric is the medium for acting on the formlessness of the world, to make it a place of life. The task for Dante is to apply virtue to the words, so that the power of words does not prompt crimes, but instead promotes honor: a just state, a true soul.

Dante hears in Ulysses' words hypnotic figures of speech and decides to "rein in [his] own genius." Ulysses' high language is another symptom of never knowing when to stop. Dante realizes that he must curb his own poet's faculty, in case it too is a symptom of madness. Poetry, said Plato, is inspired madness. Dante's next canto, *Inferno* 27, begins his reining in. Ulysses' smooth talk is replaced by hypotheticals, in the talk of Count Guido da Montefeltro, lord of Romagna, another victim of Boniface VIII's ambition:

> "*S'i' credesse che mia risposta fosse*
> *a persona che mai tornasse al mondo,*
> *questa fiamma staria sanza più scosse;*
>
> *ma però che già mai di questo fondo*
> *non tornò vivo alcun, s'i' odo il vero,*
> *sanza tema d'infamia ti rispondo. . . ."*

> "If I thought that my answer were to one who might ever
> return to the world, this flame should
> shake no more;
>
> but since none ever did return alive from this
> depth, if what I hear be true, without fear of
> infamy I answer you. . . ."

(27.61–66; trans. Wicksteed)

The time has come when Dante can use language for no other end than truth: he will come back alive and bear witness. Craftiness closes around the dead like tongues of fire, and one becomes invisible to others. The theft and shrinkage and decay of the soul happen by misuse of language, until the soul grows so small that it can be confined within the narrow flame of a firefly. Ulysses has dwindled to a spark.

Poets, says Thomas Aquinas, are liars. "Not I," Dante responds. Brunetto had done the right sort of thing in the wrong sort of way. Dante's own explanation of why he wrote the *Comedy* is "to teach you how to make better prayers."

And from here on, in Purgatory—the mountain Ulysses longed to reach—that is what Dante does.

★

FOR SOME, A shipwreck is definitive. For others, it is a prelude to a new life. *Com' altrui piacque.*

Ulysses' journey, as Homer told the story, was circular. The hero returned home, to Greece and to the afterlife, the same person as when he left. Dante's is a journey of change. He wants to be free of what had imprisoned him, a world of relative truths, cycles of loves, not love. For him, the journey is the poem: the ultimate objective of the pilgrim is to become the poet and gain poetic knowledge. Purely philosophical excursions do not please an Other. Dante's descent into Hell enables him to reach the shore Ulysses was only able to make out in the distance.

Dante builds *Inferno* 26 into *Purgatorio* 26 and *Paradiso* 26. Each of the three Cantos 26 echo each other, yet advance the discovery of how to please God, Fortune, fate. The three 26's form a circle that breaks repetition: a circle that moves forward like an arrow. *Purgatorio* 26 advances *Inferno* 26. *Paradiso* 26 reveals ideas of expression that transcend speech, time and desire. The marvelous 26's create a work that is not merely written but built. They have architectural form. This is the work of a poet who trusts more than words. For Dante, words are things; this is a work of words built on geometric principles as cathedral builders work in stone.

Humility, love of fate, perception of grace: these please the souls in Purgatory, and they please an Other. The most farsighted souls of the Inferno would leap at a chance to make up for the destruction they caused "while in the form of bones and pulp my mother gave me," as Count Guido is on the verge of doing:

"... *l'opere mie*
non furon leonine, ma di volpe.

Li accorgimenti e le coperte vie
io seppi tutte, e sì menai lor arte,
ch'al fine de la terra il suono uscie.

Quando mi vidi giunto in quella parte
di mia etade, ove ciascun dovrebbe
calar le vele e raccoglier le sarte,

ciò che pria mi piacëa, allor m'increbbe . . ."

"... my deeds were not those
of the lion but of the fox.

All wiles and covert ways I knew; and used
the art of them so well, that to the ends
of the earth the sound went forth.

When I saw myself come to that period
   of my age at which every one should lower
   sails and gather in his ropes

that which before had pleased me, grieved me . . ."

(Inferno 27.74–82; trans. Wicksteed)

Purgatorio 1 ends with the line *"humile pianta"*: Virgil picks up a reed to tie around Dante's waist, confirming his humility—"as pleased an Other." The souls in *Purgatorio* 26 don't just submit to punishment. They love to be corrected. They have come to embrace their fate in Saint Francis's sense (not in Nietzsche's): *amor fati*. The equivalent today would be meeting a terrible crisis as an opportunity to discover something new about oneself and human nature. Marco Lombardo doesn't want to take too long away from the pitchy smoke he has to breathe (*Purgatorio* 16); Guido del Duca says he'd rather cry than talk (*Purgatorio* 14). Here penitents are nourished by their time in the flame that tormented Ulysses; it burns off their chaff, their weight and waste.

In *Purgatorio* 26, instead of Ulysses in *Inferno* 26, the soul of the poet Guido Guinizelli talks to Dante directly, without Virgil's translating. He was the most famous poet before Dante to write in the *lingua volgare*.

Guinizelli is stuck in Purgatory because he was subject to unchecked lust—wanderings of a Ulyssean kind. But Guinizelli repents and hopes to reach Paradise. He tells Dante that the souls here cry out their own crimes. The souls are being distilled to their essential genius, in which language creates reality. Dante defends his art through these cantos in *Purgatorio*. He promises to pray for

Guido. Guido, having gratefully declined Dante's offer to rehabilitate his fame, begs Dante for merely a short prayer on his behalf, then draws back and disappears willingly into the flames: "To give place to someone else, whoever might be nearest"—*altrui*—"he vanished through the flames, like a fish going to the bottom through the water" (lines 133–35).

*

WHO IS THIS being "an Other"? *Altrui:* from the Latin *alter,* meaning "other of the two," from which come "alter" (change from one thing to another), "altruism" (to serve another), and "altercate" (to fight another). But why did Dante not name "the other"? Did he mean to suggest that God was not the only One? Or that the other was "Papa Satan," whose pleasure one must not serve? It remains a mystery.

Dante doesn't ever talk about God's violence. But the sense of it is everywhere. When he gets as far as he can go, to the top of Paradiso, Dante with the sun under his feet looks back at the earth and sees, even from that vast distance, horrendous violence. Two points stand out: the shore where Jupiter, disguised as a bull, raped Europa in the east, and in the west he sees the *"varco folle"*—the "mad voyage"—of Ulysses. Europe was founded in the violence of the gods, and in almost perfect symmetry, the epic hero Ulysses stages a violent transgression of the boundaries of Europe. Dante has reimagined Homer's heroic Ulysses as a ruined Captain Vivaldi. The tragic hero opens a path into secret and forbidden spaces. Yet Dante knows there are other vast spaces of knowledge and possible pathways leading to them (*Paradiso* 27. 79–87).

And God—an Other—isn't He the one who put these dreams into old Ulysses' mind? Just as God kept Levi from his mountains? Who is this Another who demands his own pleasure?

That Dante will discover in *Paradiso* 26, the soul's lesson in ambition, prompted by Ulysses, now brought full circle: the flame appears as light, not heat. Dante, who has been blinded by the light of Paradise, intellectually dazzled, has his sight restored. He expresses his love for God. He explains that he has made the journey in order to see Beatrice again: "let healing come to the eyes which were portals when she entered in the fire with which I burn."

Beatrice turns her eyes upon Dante, and he is immediately endowed with perfect sight. She tells Dante that he is wrapped in the same light as Adam, the first human, the "primal power."

What this means to those who have walked the track of the marvelous 26's is that Dante has by this point overcome his fury at the unjust sentencing and recognizes that it had a providential design. *Amor fati*. As pleased Another: he is now choosing the fate that has been chosen for him. Submission to a greater will: this is chief among the qualities of love, which is the most humbling emotion. Dante begins to see himself as the locus of history, his sentence as providential as the expulsion of the Jews from Egypt. That was a triumph of the Jews: a sacred death which one must experience. It is a colossal readjustment of his vision. Dante is no more simply a just man. *He is a man who accepts injustice as a factor in his own salvation.* In return for pleasing Another, one finds pleasure. Ulysses refuses the light of grace and goes to terrifying extremes. Augustine defines "the Happy Life" as "gratuitous," meaning literally lived by grace, waiting for the surprises that come in the darkest times, grateful for them.

★

NICCOLÒ MACHIAVELLI, whose long argument with *Inferno* 26 led him to write *The Prince,* abandoned grace as a form of power. Dante is his fictive interlocutor. John Freccero has said: "Machiavelli knew every inch of Dante." He agreed with Dante that "Virtue conquers Fortune." But Machiavelli believed that power is acquired by manipulation. If we are successful, we *think* it's because we are good, not *that* we are good. Luck has favored us. Niccolò imagines "an Other" is a woman, and he suggests to readers of *The Prince* that they treat her violently: "It is necessary to beat her and jolt her." Fortune will betray the ambitious Prince unless he dominates her. *Astuzia,* astuteness, life-destroying for Ulysses, becomes a valued quality in the Renaissance. Machiavelli is astute.

As the poets reached the deepest depths of Hell, the circle of the archfiends of mankind, Brutus, Cassius and Judas—the first two betrayed Caesar; the other, Christ—they entered the icy regions, where the burn comes from the chill of Lucifer's wings beating the air to a bludgeoning wind. Dante grabs onto the hide of "the Great Worm of Evil / which bores through the world" (34.108–9). Dante and Virgil descend to the very bottom, using the tangled hair on Lucifer's thighs as a ladder. They pass the center of gravity to emerge from Hell. A long climb from the earth's core to the foothills of Mount Purgatory awaits them. They continue, up the banks of the River Lethe, whose waters breed forgetfulness. Finally,

> . . . i 'vidi de le cose belle
> che porta 'l ciel, per un pertugio tondo.
> E quindi uscimmo a riveder le stelle.

I saw

through a round opening, some of those things of beauty
     Heaven bears. It was from there
that we emerged, to see—once more—the stars.

(34.137–39; trans. Mandelbaum)

. . . The tracks of an Other.

Once Dante reaches this point—when *Inferno* is finished and the climb up Mount Purgatory has begun—fortune has found him. *Inferno* will be read by everyone, eclipsing the two bestsellers, Marco Polo's *Voyages* and Jean de Meun's tale of romantic love, *Roman de la Rose*. Dante at last has a voice and an audience. Perhaps the sweetest vindication: Ser Francesco, a Florentine scribe, please note, wrote out a hundred copies of *Inferno* in order to provide dowries for his daughters. Dante has passed an important test: he is seen as God's scribe. But the test is not over. As poet and diplomat Paul Claudel will write in the early decades of the twentieth century: "The mystery of history is that God writes straight with crooked lines." That style is manifest on Mount Purgatory.

PART III

Purgatorio (1308-12)

. . . *e tanto d'uno in altro vaneggiai,*
che li occhi per vaghezza ricopersi,
e 'l pensamento in sogno trasmutati.

. . . *E come questa imagine rompeo*
sé per sé stessa, a guisa d'una bulla
cui manca l'acqua sotto qual si feo. . . .

. . . *così l'imaginar mio cadde giuso* . . .

. . . I was so drawn from random thought
to thought that, wandering in mind, I shut
my eyes, transforming thought on thought to dream

. . . and when this image shattered of itself
just like a bubble that has lost the water
beneath which it was formed

. . . so my imagination fell away

(*Purgatorio* 18.143–45; 17.31–34, 43;

trans. Mandelbaum)

CHAPTER 7

Virgin Discoveries

DANTE IS ABOUT TO DISCOVER THAT GOOD AND EVIL, genius and stupidity, have one and the same source, which is love. In Purgatory he must journey upward and purge himself of hunger, thirst and longing—a considerable effort when there is so much to want and he is so much in need, in this the true child of his times.

*

LOVE WAS in the air and so was madness, and they were revising the map of Europe. A mystic saint named Hadewijch spoke of desire as "inseparable assaults of satiety and hunger. Love may devour eternity," she prophesied. Nowhere did this appear more likely than in Cordova in 1290, where a student of how the world works, Moses de León, transcribed the thoughts of the grand master of Jewish philosophy, Simeon bar Yochai. De León, living at the end of the Crusades, wrote down the secret visions imparted to his followers by Simeon, who had for a decade hidden in a cave with his son waiting for the First Crusade to pass with its frenzy of messianic devotion. In his cave, Simeon had meditated on God. When he finally emerged, he observed that the fighting had ended but nothing had changed.

He walked through the fields, growing increasingly distraught by the sight of peasants treating each other cruelly, knights bereft of ideals, the sweet beauty of the troubadours, their tender songs destroyed, and everywhere toil and anger and expressions of woe. Because his mind had become pure in the effort of seeking truth and beauty, no gap existed between his thoughts and his deeds. His eyes burn every object that meet their disdain. God is outraged by this, he tells us. "Go back into the cave, Simeon!" he hears him say. "Stop destroying my world."

Chastened and frightened, Simeon returned to the darkness and to his imagination. When de León wrote these teachings down for the first time, he called Simeon's visions of a better life the Zohar—the Book of Splendor—a mystical tract on how to transcend time and space. De León made available what had heretofore been secret teachings passed down through the ages in hushed tones of cabalistic masters on how to raise oneself to a godly level. But the Zohar's author claimed something new: "The pillars of the world have discussed the secrets of their words," he proclaimed. Simeon had seen the face of God and declared it a she: Shekhina. Columbus finding land or Galileo discovering the voyage of celestial bodies could not have been more impressed with the object of his sight than was Simeon bar Yochai.

Here she was, the hidden knowledge that fools denied existed—better than the fleshy vision of God Abelard had known. Shekhina was a vision more intellectual yet more fanciful, and certainly more romantic. This was a part of God who loved the soul rather than commanded it.

To write of Paradise from inside of it lay beyond the greatest powers of the greatest poets and visionaries. But the Zohar launched an assault on rabbinic teaching, so rational and legalistic.

The sensuous, soulful Shekhina became a *cause célèbre*. The Zohar was copied. It traveled to Tuscany, where it focused the desire for initiation into these *mysteries* upon a quasi-erotic object. The path toward transcendence grew inflamed and otherworldly at the same time. One sought a transport, *ecstasy*, out of the self to the other; an ardent cherishing, *zeal*, of another; a melting, *liquefaction*, so that the heart is unfrozen and open to be entered; a longing in absence, *languor*, heat in pursuit, *fervor*, and enjoyment in presence, *fruition*. In this, there is an all-at-once wholeness and timelessness that reflects the *total simultaneity* of eternity—a complete fulfillment of activity without satiety beyond any mortal satisfaction, hobbled by the fact that "they that drink shall yet thirst." This was not a work on love, or rather, it was on the love of God: on the state of feeling blessed, or loved. This sounds like the psychological idea of sublimation: the lifting of lower energy to higher ends. The Zohar's Shekhina bore a similarity to Beatrice, the woman of Dante's eternal fascination.

Shekhina was born in the Christian world the year Beatrice died, and Dante, who considered all dates meaningful, might have believed her soul lighted up the rabbi's cave. As he knew from Virgil, when exceptional women perish, their souls live on even more beautifully. Iris the rainbow goddess has to cut the last strand of life in Virgil's queen, Dido, as the soul hates to leave a charming body.

He must find a language in which he too may see and speak as if time were no barrier; for this, Dante has endured the Inferno. He wants to be able to tell Beatrice—and say of her—what never could be said in the thin grey language of everyday discourse. For that he does not simply need art; he needs the moral courage of the artist, and a vision of love that transports him beyond fear. With *Purgatorio*, the second phase of his self-education begins.

Purgatorio, the second canticle of *The Divine Comedy,* is a work on the art of loss: how to make everything out of nothing.

At the foothills of Mount Purgatory, Dante considered his fate to be like the Jews' in the book of Exodus; he was lost in the desert of Tuscany, wandering, waiting for a messianic sign that he might come home. The Jews were "shadowy prefaces of the truth" for Dante. The church too showed a grudging respect for Simeon bar Yochai's vision. The Jews were considered heretics, but the church fathers treated their mysticism the way a cat treats a mouse: with enormous attention. The Zohar had gone further in embracing the feminine mysteries than had the church. Eros— desire—possession, leads toward God, not away. No one had been as bold as Simeon in the pursuit of a larger, brighter and more dangerous world, dangerous defined as "bent on divine knowledge."

Though he didn't know it, the cave-dweller had given Dante a great gift: he had given him back his dead Beatrice, reborn in the image of the Shekhina. This was the new Beatrice who would become his guide, confessor and teacher in Purgatory.

*

DANTE HAD BEGUN writing *Purgatorio* by 1308. Historian Flavio Biondo (d. 1463) places Dante in Forlì in this year, a speck of a town known as a place to nurse a drink forever, as there is nothing else to do there. He bases it on a passage in *Purgatorio* 24, lines 31–33:

Vidi messer Marchese, ch'ebbe spazio
già di bere a Forlì con men secchezza,
e si fu tal, che non si sentì sazio.

I saw Messer Marchese, who once had
more ease, less dryness, drinking at Forlì
and yet could never satisfy his thirst.

(trans. Mandelbaum)

Dante says he is like a sick sleeper tossing from side to side, uncomfortable everywhere he settles. He will move to Lucca, probably after a stay in Bologna. He will perhaps stop for a time in Paris to lose himself among strangers studying philosophy and theology. Then, in 1310, Henry VII of Luxembourg will march into Italy in an effort to rule it, raising Dante's hopes of peace and the lifting of his exile. Emperors had for centuries avoided their Italian responsibilities, and Henry's expedition will call Dante back to Italy. In Purgatory, he will not get one good night's sleep. At night, he dreams of an eagle, a siren and a host of women. He climbs the steep mountain by day.

Souls who will undergo cleansing arrive in Purgatory in "a boat so light, so quick / that nowhere did the water swallow it" (2.40–41). On each terrace, a thirst or hunger is purged—trans-formed—into a timeless desire. Pride, envy, wrath, sloth, greed, gluttony and lust distract from the desire that breeds no further hunger. That is perfection, bliss, an end to the wandering eye and spirit. Dante is given the chance to make a clean start, to purge his mistakes and doomful habits. His own desire is excited by the fact that Beatrice is so near. It has been years since he saw her in Florence—ten, according to the telescoped time frame of the poem.

*

"LOOK BEHIND YOU," Beatrice will say to Dante when he reaches the uppermost level of Purgatory, midway between the Inferno and Paradise. She will take him to his goal: entry into the mind of God. He will look back at that point and see the world disappear. Revealed to him at last will be the stored magic of the universe for which he has made his dangerous journey.

This begs the central mystery of the *Comedy* and of Dante's journey: Why does Beatrice, a woman who died too young to have gained significant experience or knowledge, show Dante— and us—a realm few seekers find? And why this young woman, who was married to a banker, a usurer in Dante's view? Why does the great Virgil address her, in Canto 2 of *Inferno*, as if she were the goddess of philosophy, she alone the means through whom one can escape the circle of life's generation and corruption?

From the perspective of Purgatory, Virgil is merely preparation. The journey through Hell under Virgil's guidance teaches human limits. Beatrice will lead Dante to see where beauty and meaning lie. She will show him a life unlike the one for which Virgil has prepared him: In Purgatory he sees the limits of art and the imagination. He will need to curb art to find a force greater than imagination.

Dantisti need to know why the souls with the best chance of arriving in Paradise define themselves in female terms—and why they must go through Purgatory to get there. Fifty years before the Zohar appeared, chess masters had added the figure of the Queen to the game, and new roles allowed men to weep and women to take charge of households. But the rise of a dominant female god from the shadows of heresy represented a major shift in the history of creativity.

The story of the search for self and immortality takes a sharp

turn now toward truth and beauty as twin qualities. The humanism of the Renaissance may owe its very existence to the female
god whom the Zohar named Shekhina, Dante would name Beatrice and others would call the Virgin, Mary, mother of God.

*

THE MOST EROTIC thrill-seekers of the High Middle Ages
were the mystic theologians. The scribe of the Zohar was advancing the claims of a monk who had experienced severe erotic afflic-
tions: St. Bernard of Clairvaux, as he would come to be called.
Bernard had gone looking for the purest light of vision as a young
man. When he didn't find it in Paris with young men he considered decadent, he headed for Cîteaux in Burgundy in 1115. He
selected this spot because it was so dreary and barren that he
could obtain no nourishment except by sucking on beech leaves. It
was known as "the valley of wormwood." Bernard had carefully
prepared himself for this choice. He tried to reach such a level of
abstraction that he lost nearly all physical sense. Food had no taste
for him. His eyes saw nothing. He ate congealed blood thinking
it was butter and drank oil for water and never noticed whether
his monastic cell had one window or two. The old monasteries
by this time had become rich and luxurious. Bernard's became
famous for its renunciation and poverty.

At one point in his young career, as he was praying for knowledge and virtue before a painting of the Virgin Mary, the image
pressed its breast and dropped on the lips of her servant three
drops of the milk that had nourished the baby Jesus. Those three
drops of milk altered history. Bernard became Mary's evangelist.
He rose in power throughout Europe, mounting big campaigns

of building Cistercian monasteries—ninety-three in all, drawing up the rules of the Knights Templar, forging peace when possible to advance the ambitions of Pope Innocent II, and fomenting religious warfare, particularly the ill-fated Second Crusade. It is said that his greatness lies in his energy, not his intellect. He also built churches to Mary at a time when worship of the Virgin was unrecognized by the church hierarchy. Much of the ancient ritual devoted to her survived in an underground form: she was praised as marah (brine) and mor (myrrh), recalling two of the gifts of the Magi.

"Theology" is another word for "imagination." And theology had been hostage to disputation. But Bernard's version of religion emphasized desire, not logic. While Bernard's charisma spread Catholicism forcefully, adopting the presence of Mary turned out to be a brilliant move. She transformed Catholicism from a religion of terror, of crucifixions and witch hunts, into a religion of mercy and love. And Bernard would end up in Dante's vision of Heaven way up at the top of the mystic rose of Paradise. The Virgin became the sinless, giving, feminine principle throughout Europe. She was housed in secrecy no more. The rough men of the guilds, even the blaspheming heroes of barracks and battlefields, found solace and genius in meeting her gaze in frescoes and paintings. She is not just an image; she becomes a mirror. Mystics like Bernard advise followers to "incarnate the Son in their own hearts." All people could participate in the Incarnation; they too could gestate an idea, a dream, a vision, and it too could change the world. Christ's suffering was humanity's suffering, the church fathers had long preached. Now, Bernard insisted that Mary was the vehicle of transformation.

Bernard saw no contradiction in maintaining that it would

be easier to catch the devil by the tail than to resist a woman's charms, and at the same time acting as the chief accomplice in helping the Virgin assume the role of mediatrix of grace. Medievalist Henry Adams, surveying Europe's growth from the perspective of the nineteenth century, said that devotion to the Virgin became more consequential in building civilization than the "dynamo." Muscle power and technology served the faith and miracle she stirred. Vast sums of money were raised to build churches that were dedicated to her. Mothers invoked her name to cure their sick babies. As a symbol, she is fertile and virginal at once; orderly and righteous, plain but ecstatic. All pure knights of the mind consider her the symbol of their own desire.

Bernard will preach that with the fall of Adam "man lost his goodness but not his greatness." He will write sermons on the salvation of kisses and the charm of women's breasts and deliver these messages with such force that parishioners will sweat in their pews. "I kiss you with the kisses of my mouth," he thunders from the pulpit. He comes to be known as the mellifluous doctor—Doctor Honey (*melli*) Breasts (*fluous,* or flowing). "The superior helps others out of love," he proclaims, "the inferior out of necessity." "It is necessary not only to know but also to love." Otherwise "a kiss's enlightenment" only "puffs one up."

Bernard was driven by ideas and imagination: wars of religion and grand schemes of spiritual empire and church-building. When Bernard preaches that love is stronger than death, he arouses his listener's disbelief at first. But thanks in large part to the example of Mary, it proves true.

On the one hand, the masters of faith, the trend setters, were indulging erotic and spiritual visions, suppressing their sexuality, we might say with twenty-first-century eyes, so that they could focus undistracted on their union with the mysterious world. On the other hand, with the rise of the money economy, life was becoming softer. They could begin to imagine life as an art. Fate could be shaped: that was the idea of Purgatory.

Purgatory was an idea that swept the imagination of Tuscany with the rise of the bourgeois and the working-class communes. It was of particular interest to members of professions that were held in contempt or regarded as suspect, such as the barber-surgeons who worked with the body and blood, but also usurers and merchants, the *inhonesta mercimonia,* who were building wealth and concerned with their reputations after death.

By 1300, Purgatory's invention as a cultural and social space was complete. Before that time, souls went to Hell or Heaven; Jesus descended into Hell and then went straight to Heaven after three days. When a person knows his life will not end with death, he undergoes a tremendous change. Purgatory offered a second chance at salvation.

Purgatory's discovery coincided with that of an economic order that desired a middle ground in which to bivouac. The logical, mathematical concept of "intermediacy" is an idea closely bound up with the profound changes in the social and intellectual reality of the High Middle Ages. Suddenly there are middle classes and a third order of lay friars that arise between the clergy and the laity. Purgatory represents the new middle class's focus on spiritual development.

For Dante, it becomes a real place. Purgatory is a school for molding one's life into a work of art: truth and beauty combined and undimmed by acts of stupidity—to Dante, cupidity. In Hell, morality or ethics were dominant forces. In Purgatory, power lies in aesthetics. Ethics is the work of judgments, narrow and harsh.

Beauty, aesthetics, are choices inspired by grace. In Purgatory the seeker sees that the face of God is feminine, not the tyrannical face of the father, or the son as the moral judge. It is a face Moses was not permitted to see on Sinai; when God passed before him, he would only show Moses his back.

God himself, said the Zohar, had to make space for the world's creation, which he did by breathing in or shrinking. Dante will do the same. As an exile, he seems to have little to his name. Now he embarks on the effort of losing even more. What more can he rid himself of? In this sense especially, Purgatory is a world of women. Male heroes of myth gain prestige and honor as they oppose evil. Female heroes follow the opposite course: their reputation is not based on gain but on overcoming loss—of children, family, beauty and status, until they are emptied, pure and virginal—the essence of being human.

That is the design Dante and Virgil discover as they pass the guardian of the mountain, the Roman orator Cato, who killed himself to save his moral virtue. Cato will let them breach the secrets of this realm he guards so vigilantly on one condition. To enter, Dante must undergo his first purgation. He must wash off the dirt and darkness of Hell. Only then will he be fit to stand in this new light, the first he has seen since he entered the dark forest at the beginning of *Inferno*. The light of Purgatory turns out to be the star of Venus, the planet of love. Dante is in love, and it is a quality of light that "brought a smile to the whole of the east" (1.20).

*

PIETAS—PITY / PIETY—in antiquity was a martial virtue. In Dante, it becomes feminine in quality, as in Michelangelo's statue two hundred years later: a woman with the body of her grown, dying son across her lap. Something very dramatic had happened between these two notions, and it happened for Dante most explicitly: a woman who is the mortal equal of a god. Dante may have entered Santa Maria in Trastevere to pray before the strange and beautiful Pietro Cavallini mosaics completed just before the end of the thirteenth century. He would have seen the female god prominently in this humble church, a structure built over the shattered ancient temple to the Egyptian goddess Isis.

Cavallini created his visions in shattered glass tesserae in this church. It shocked even this neighborhood, long home to sailors, prostitutes and merchants—the rough trade. When Caravaggio paints his scene of a dying Mary (*Death of the Virgin*) in 1603, he will use as his model a prostitute who died by throwing herself into the Tiber at this exact point. There was no telling what one would find in thirteenth-century Trastevere. On quiet nights the devil was reportedly seen on a head of lettuce being eaten by a nun.

The churches named for Mary were meant to remind people that these piles were one step toward Paradise. Nearly every great church built after Bernard was dedicated to Mary. Many are mountainous white matrons in marble crinolines. Sailors brought Mary to their ports. The name, says the maker of the first dictionary, the seventh-century scholar Isidore of Seville, means "a drop of water from the sea" (*stilla maris*), and "drop" (*stilla*) became "star" (*stella*). Mary became the star guiding the ship of the faithful. One can imagine the sailors may have favored these medieval beauties like little boys returning to their mothers' skirts. When Beatrice meets Dante in upper Purgatory, she makes her "bearded schoolboy" cry as if he were a child who betrayed her love with other women and unworthy pastimes.

Dante would certainly have seen the Santa Maria in Trastevere Cavallini frescoes by 1300, on his way into Rome to meet Boniface or soon after as an outcast. As such, he would not have stood out in this part of Rome. He would have seen the exterior mosaic, crafted partly in tesserae of gold, the first public image in which Mary suckles baby Jesus with a naked breast. He would have walked past the sarcophagi which form a wall at the entrance and read in the etchings how this first Roman church consecrated to Mary spoke the polyglot of the dead: a Star of David carved on one marble tomb, a bird of the Holy Spirit scratched out hurriedly on another, and the wavy lines drawn in a third signifying the combs Roman athletes used to brush the excess oil from their bodies before an athletic competition.

Inside the church, Cavallini crafted images of the Virgin sitting like a Roman wife beside Jesus. The marvel is that she is his equal in size and importance, *but also his creator:* Jesus has Mary's face; he is clearly in her image. God chose a woman to bring forth a god. Dante will remark upon this fertile paradox when he sees Mary in Paradise that she is "the daughter of her son." The doctors of the church railed about the devil being housed in a woman, but here in Cavallini's vision was proof of the opposite. Still, the real shock lay in Mary's human beauty as the artist expressed it. The women in Purgatory are described as beautiful. "As pleased Another," the phrase that resounded heavily in Hell, here shifts. *Piacque* means "pleasing," beauty that transcends 'nature or art' " (31.50).

Virgin fever led other builders to produce monuments. These took the form of Gothic cathedrals. "Conceived" is the important notion. One could give birth to a fully fleshed idea. Just like God. The new realm that took shape was the Middle Kingdom, Purgatory. It embodied suffering not in and for itself but as a transformation, a rebirth.

The body was a womb. The popularization of the Virgin shifted the hold of the ancient classical view of sensuous bodies and perfect proportion. Medieval artists portrayed people as rigid, staring into space, seeming not to belong to each other. The change represented a protest. People wanted to escape to a higher realm. They left love of the human body for flight from this world. The Greek word for "athlete," *asketes,* had become the word for "ascetic." The High Middle Ages constituted "a wrestling school of the spirit," said the eleventh-century contemplative Peter Damian, whose fame in his time rested on the introduction of fantastic forms of severe self-discipline, including flagellation. "The frailty of the flesh contends with the powers of the air," he said.

Church art was meant to edify spiritually. The thirteenth-century man did not "find himself" by casting off inhibiting patterns but by adopting appropriate ones. For moderns, the goal of development is to become an excellent adult. For Dante, it was to find a likeness to God, built on a model found in the inner self. Here in Cavallini's mosaics, the face of God was indelibly Mary's and female.

*

MOST LITERARY MYTHS are father quests. Aeneas searches for his fatherland. Jesus returns to God the Father. Rarely are secret quests searches for the mother figure. Odysseus takes ten years to return home to Penelope; meanwhile she has her own hidden Homeric journey, the Penelopiad. Achilles hides himself among women and takes the name of a woman. The oldest mythic Celtic warrior Cuchulain slayed thousands in the cause of Irish freedom, then begged entry into a school run by a woman fighter, Scathach. Dante acquires a father early on, Virgil. But Purgatory is a mother quest: the object first Beatrice, and then the Virgin.

Dante may have had one more initiation into the feminine mysteries before he began *Purgatorio* around 1308. In the fall of that year, he arrived at the abbey of the convent of Santa Croce, an order of the Hermits of St. Augustine, to drop off his manuscript of *Inferno* with the abbot for safekeeping. It was at a time when the feminine mysteries had the neighborhood of Santa Croce astir, for a very good reason.

In August, the abbot of the monastery, Ilario, had opened the rib cage of the second abbess, Clare of Montefalco, who had died the night before. Ilario would later testify to the legates of the pope's committee investigating her possible canonization that Clare had appeared to him in the morning, tapped his shoulder, and said, "Look and see if I am beautiful." He opened her chest and observed her heart. Autopsies were rare (the corpses of ardent Christians were often boiled and their parts distributed), and Ilario was not looking for the cause of death, but the secret of Clare's amazing life.

What Ilario saw in the glistening inscape of organs were a crucifix, a whip, a pillar, a crown of thorns, nails, a lance and a rod with a sponge. All the tools of Christ's last passion were lodged there. Such, if found in a patient's chest by pathologists today, would probably be read as signs of a fatal fatty buildup. Ilario and other witnesses were satisfied that this trove constituted beauty. The church would canonize Clare a mere 537 years later. Clare had transformed herself into a work of art. She had done it through love, by making herself an incarnation of the most commanding idea of her time.

Beatrice, in her bodiless form, will cry to Dante, much as Clare did: *"Riguarda qual son io"*—"Look at what I am." He too will for the first time see her true beauty, and more importantly he will not be afraid of what beauty does to him.

*

DANTE ENTERING PURGATORIO has begun a new journey: *morphosis.* The word "formation" is the word for "education": philosophers showing the way to the light. In Hell, change was not possible. Here change, transformation, is the principle of beauty.

Hell has been a breakdown of the illusions with which people comfort themselves. The Inferno is a deconstruction. In *Inferno,* all the great heroes are savagely attacked, from Cavalcanti and Farinata to Frederick II, monarch of Sicily. But the principle object of deconstruction is Dante himself.

In *Purgatorio,* the heroes pare themselves down to their feminine souls. They captivate Dante with the qualities of virgin genius, and he too begins to wonder how blessings and grace fill a person's soul. Manfred, the favorite son of Frederick II, identifies himself with the good women in his family. He has a father in Hell, Frederick, but a grandmother in Heaven as well as a loving daughter on earth.

".... *Io son Manfredi,*
nepote di Costanza imperadrice;
ond' io priego che, quando tu riedi,

vada a mia bella figlia, genitrice
  de l'onor di Cicilia e d'Aragona,
  e dichi 'l vero a lei, s'altro si dice.

.... *Or le bagna la pioggia e move il vento*

  . . .

Per lor maladizion sì non si perde,
  che non possa tornar, l'etterno amore,
  mentre che la speranza ha fior del verde."

"I am Manfred, grandson
of the Empress Constance; I beg you
therefore, when you have returned again,

  to go to my beautiful daughter, mother
of the kings of Sicily and Aragon—
tell her the truth . . .
now rain bathes my bones . . .

  there is no one
so lost that the eternal love cannot
return—as long as hope keeps the least bit of green."

  (3.112ff.; trans. Merwin and Mandelbaum)

Elsewhere in Purgatory, Dante's fellow poet and forerunner
Guido Guinizelli is compared to a mother whose twin sons arrive

in time to save her from execution in *Purgatorio* 26.94–96. Men do women's bidding. Even more, Dante will find that there is no distinction in sex in eternity: man can be spoken of as female, woman as male. Piccarda, a woman, is addressed by Dante in the masculine as *ben creato spirito*. The word *indonna* in *Paradiso* 7.13–14 means "take control of, rules over" (from *dominare*) and the relationship to "lady" is significant.

The mystery known as feminine—the grail which seekers believed was erotic or, to use their word, magical—was beauty. With every purgation a soul or *anima* prayed for by a woman becomes lighter, more the embodiment of grace. Medievals have been accused of reducing the beautiful to the useful or the moral. Far from doing this, however, they gave moral values an aesthetic foundation.

"Give beauty back," the late-nineteenth-century Jesuit poet Gerard Manley Hopkins wrote, based on Dante's statement in *Purgatory* 15 that goods should be shared the way light is shared by mirrors. The examples are all of reciprocity: of giving back. "As when a ray of light leaps from the water or from a mirror to the opposite direction, ascending at an angle similar to that at which it descends . . ." The light is so bright, the poet must avert his eyes and wonders what it would be like to look without squinting at the beauty hidden in the light.

Beauty, said one of the great mystics in Dante's time, Dionysius the Areopagite, was one of the ninety-four names of God, but beauty had no special connection with the fine arts. It implied a pleasing relationship, spiritual or material, moral or physical, artistic or natural, limited or vast. The arts became disciplines, even "astringents," in the Middle Ages, and pleasure was only to a limited degree connected with artistic enjoyment.

Beauty came from viewing one's life as larger than oneself. One is a part of a whole, just as memories are not encoded in our minds but everywhere in us, our muscles, our taste buds, our body temperature. Contact with beauty requires us to give up our imagined position at the center—a radical decentering or "unselfing." To purge the self of deforming ego can happen only in the presence of beauty, when one becomes self-forgetting. The effort in the service of protecting or advancing the self is now freed to be in the service of something else—a "bystander" or a "donor." When we feel ourselves in this role, we come closer to feeling equal to what we observe or experience. Before a great work of art—a canvas, play, text—one enlarges with the thrill, though one is "only" an observer.

This is how aesthetics trumps ethics. One doesn't choose based on narrow ideas of behavior, but guided by rapture. Augustine said that beauty is lifesaving, "a plank amid waves of the sea."

The medievals believed that there is more beauty and wonder in this cosmos than its opposite. "Existence," says philosopher Richard Rorty, "is endurable only as an esthetic fact."

The beauty Dante discovers through the feminine mysteries is not simply what twentieth-century philosopher Ludwig Wittgenstein described as something the hand wants to grasp when the eye sees it. It's the beauty that reveals the order of the world. As he climbs the mountain, Dante learns that the soul loves to receive sensations that agree with it and rejects sensations that are unsuitable and harmful. Beauty presents the best-integrated picture. One can touch and taste things only partially, but mostly in sight, and next in hearing, one grasps what is present in its frame and meaning. From here on, all Dante's decisions will be made by this standard.

*

THEN WHY IS Beatrice "the soul more worthy than I am," as Virgil says? She is the *mistificaccio* in Dante's life, his savior. "Mystification" was a good word in the Middle Ages. It broadened people's perspectives rather than narrowed them down.

Beatrix, meaning "happy, blessed." Dante makes of his first love a prophecy of justice and love. If she is in the world, it is possible for all things to be good and great. "To Dante, the good and great, the foundation for love, is the concept of the august Holy Roman Empire reaching out in ever-widening influence to include the globe . . . under the rule of the One Monarch." In the age of iron, when evil dominates the world, Ovid said, the virgin abandons the blood-soaked earth. And so when Beatrice dies, Dante decides to go in search of her through the underground and conquer death, as the greek singer Orpheus did, as Christ did, as artists do.

She becomes the image of his soul, his code for love and wisdom, sweetness and greatness: combinations we have lost in our time when genius defines grief and romantic suffering. Dante would have scarce compassion for depression or madness as creative virtues. Depression, sloth, was one of the seven deadly sins in a time marked by rapid change and thunderstruck love.

At first Beatrice is a woman: Dante writes a book to her memory, *La Vita Nuova,* begun in 1283 and finished in 1292. In it, he mentions her name 4 times in the prose and 19 times in the poetry. He refers to the god of love more than 100 times. Slowly she becomes more his own state of mind: he has incarnated her. She is the figure 9 who dies in the 9th hour of the 9th day in the 9th month which the perfect number (10) had completed 9 times in the century (*Vita Nuovo* 29). He makes this love a transcendence: she becomes "the glorious woman of my mind."

Beatrice is the key to Dante's ideas of beauty and its redeeming force. How can one incarnate beauty? She will tell him. He seeks the source of Beatrice's beauty as the way to God. His eyes cannot bear the divine light except as it is reflected in her eyes. When he is tired in Purgatory, love makes him climb. When he is afraid, she draws him through the fire. Twelve lines of persuasion from Virgil do nothing, but the simple words *"Tra Beatrice e te è questo muro"* do it all. She forces him to see himself as he is and to accept responsibility for what he has done. She raises him to the height of his powers and beyond; it is she who "imparadises" his mind (*Paradiso* 28.3). She is the continuing source of his power. It is through her eyes that he receives the reflected light of God that draws him upward.

Beauty shows us the third truth in Dante's cosmology: The first truth is the self-evident, that which is based on habit and experience. The second is reason. Since we don't have objectively visible truth, we have at least reasoning. But the third truth is grace— "the wings of the angel," Dante says—the imagination. If one is granted the power to behold the truth, one's senses seem shallow, but before one, a world infinitely more real opens up. Beauty (order) is the vastness of the mind of God.

Dantean Journeys

Through the last six cantos of *Purgatorio*—the summit called Earthly Paradise—only women speak to Dante. Seven of them halt "at the edge / of a dense shadow such as mountains cast /

beneath green leaves and black boughs, on cold banks" (33.109–11; Mandelbaum). They spoke as well to the director Federico Fellini. *La Dolce Vita* (The Sweet Life), he called his Purgatorio. In that classic film, the journalist Marcello Rubini wanders Italy in search of an authentic life. In the film's seven episodes, Marcello passes through a world of women, one of whom, his fiancée Emma, tells him, "You haven't the slightest idea what it means to love somebody. You have lost the right path." A film star, Sylvia, leaps with him into the Trevi Fountain, lifts her hand from the water and holds it over his head, the drops falling like a blessing, a baptism. At the close, Marcello sees a distant Beatrice who smiles at him radiantly from a place where shore and sky suggest the horizon.

"The only thing I want to know," Fellini said, "is 'Why am I here? What is my life?'" He apologized for always making the same film—of some aspect of the *Comedy*—in search of the answer.

CHAPTER 8

Number-Crunchers in Paris

THE CLOSER DANTE GETS TO THE TOP OF THE WORLD, the tougher the climb for him and for us. Taking as its focus the power of vision as it does, it is odd that *Paradiso* is Dante's most difficult canticle. "It's not poetry," declared the poet Mark Strand. Samuel Beckett thought the uniformity of the angels lining up in *Paradiso* as chilly as a cult's. Much more interesting were the denizens of Hell, each befouled in his own way. "I would have written over the gates of Heaven what is said to be written over Hell—abandon all hope ye who enter here," Beckett said. *Paradiso* is never dry, said Eliot. "It is either incomprehensible or intensely exciting." Struggling with his translation, the nineteenth-century poet Henry Wadsworth Longfellow lamented how few scholars lasted long enough in *Paradiso* to write commentaries on it. He quoted Pietro Balbi, a Renaissance Dantista, on how to find the pleasure in Dante's third empire:

> Paradise will delight those who find themselves in a somewhat similar disposition of mind to that of Dante when he was writing it: those who having in their youth lived in the world and sought happiness in it, have now arrived at maturity, old age or satiety, and seek by the means of philosophy and theology to know as far as pos-

sible of that other world on which their hopes now rest. Philosophy is the romance of the aged, and Religion is the only future history for us all.

What makes *Paradiso* so maddening yet so transforming is that it represents the final effort of the artist to transcend his powers, his education, his art and his emotions. It could not have been possible had Dante not made a separate pilgrimage outside of Italy years before he began writing this third and concluding canticle in 1316. He sees in this trip the principle by which we created beings share the same elements of all created things—a bridge, a tower, a poem—and how by following these principles one makes things that defy death and become "future history."

*

IN 1308, DANTE was a traveler who had left one shore and not yet reached the other. *Inferno* was becoming a *cause célèbre*, a *"People* magazine" of Hell: so this is where the famous and infamous of Florence ended up. Children would run up and touch the cloak of the man who wrote *Inferno*. As his fame spread, Dante spent more and more time as the guest of wealthy patrons.

To stay alive as an artist, however, Dante needed to send a message of hope for the future generations. These were the years when he wrote *Purgatorio,* 1308 through 1312. They correspond to the years of hope for peace in Italy, whose living symbol became the presumed political savior Henry VII, who was already on the march to end the civil wars in Italy. *Purgatorio* is filled with messages of hope for the suffering souls who know their trials will be rewarded. Purgatory is also the passage to Paradise, and what is

Paradise to a homeless man? Dante had to write of Paradise; and to write it, he had to experience it as surely as he had experienced Hell. It would be one more choice to risk his soul. Only those choices keep away the death-in-life feeling. In 1308, the question of where the twisting mountain will lead must have weighed on him. In 1309, a year into the writing of *Purgatorio,* a year into tasting promises, still unfulfilled, of a renewed empire, Dante left the ant heap of turmoil which was Italy and sailed from the port of Genoa to Paris, the capital city of Europe, to see what a heavenly destination might look like. Like a tourist, he is allowed a glimpse of Paradise as he climbs the mountain toward it.

Paris had long aspired to be the heir both of Jerusalem and Athens—the spiritual and artistic center of the civilized world. Dante's destination was the University of Paris, the center of learning in theology and the heavenly sciences—astronomy, astrology and light. Abelard and Héloïse named their son, conceived in rooms in the shadow of the university, Astrolabe, after the sextant that for the first time measured the light of the stars. The Romans called Paris Lutetia, City of Light—a name it bears to this day, Lutèce, in the sentiment of artists who find its light extraordinary. To medieval eyes, all things achieved unity in light. Differences are not sharper in luminescence; they are contained in it, all as one. God the Unifier's thoughts can be read in light. The rainbow was believed to be connected to the halo, and the halo to the candlelight of the soul. Scientists longed to get the rainbow into the laboratory where it could be studied. To get to Paradise, one had to know what it looked like, tasted like, felt like. For that, the University of Paris was essential. Throughout *Paradiso,* Dante will be tested on matters of light and transcendence by Beatrice—who quizzes him on everything from vows to free will, from the motion of the heavens to the existence of moon spots. He will respond to her queries—and those of Saint Peter—sounding like a student defending his thesis, with Beatrice the immortal master of the art of bliss. Dante's Parisian learning doesn't fail him.

But there is another element to his approach to Paradise, and it is the quality that truly tests his desire for perfection: his restlessness. Dante cannot settle down. There is cause for his despair, for concern that an end to needs and desires is an impossible state to attain. The love Dante has found up until Paradise has been love fascinated by death. Everything has had in it the seeds of its own destruction. That marked everyone in the *Inferno*. And in Purgatory, death and loss will be for the cause of a new beginning: namely Paradise.

Dante understood that his fate was to show up at places just as something important was ending. Rome was about to rid itself of Boniface just before Boniface got rid of Dante. He arrived at Clare's apotheosis after the autopsy. He came of age at the crest of the High Middle Ages, as feudalism was ending and the forces that had destroyed feudalism—the institutions of individuality and commerce and nation-building—were waning. Looking for peaks and timeless experiences, all he saw were ghosts, legends and the dried-up legacies of thirteenth-century accomplishments. In a way, this timing was his gift.

"Greatest works mark historical change," the Harvard classicist John Finley wrote in a peculiar syntax that suggests his own brush with the state beyond words that is Paradise. He suggests that the satisfaction and genius of *Paradiso* arrive in the form of new history-making beginnings: "The *Aeneid* expresses change from [tales of] conquest to Roman inwardness; the *Divine Comedy*, though judged a summary of the Middle Ages, yet its Italian is contrasted to Latin and its advocacy of secular as contrasted to Papal government looks to a coming age. [Similarly], Shakespeare's tragedies reflect a lost sense of the divine right of kings and the fixity of morals." Paradise may be entered only in proximity to death and loss.

Paradiso for Dante's students arrives by sacrificing knowledge and returning to one's beginnings. James Joyce freed himself from all he knew of the limitations of language in *Finnegan's Wake,* his radical work in which he invented his own language, an effort to see through the limits of artistic technique, his "old man's brief." T. S. Eliot did not achieve the absolute, as Dante did, but he came alive with an urgent sense of self-confession in his last great work, *Four Quartets,* his imitation of *Paradiso.*

"Thoughts that soar before they rise," Dante described the heights of Paradise. One thinks of the painter Titian, the consummate crafter, who in his last years found the freedom to paint the most moving works with his thumbs, an old man's vision joined to the unselfconsciousness of a child. Paradise is the last border that limits vision and art, time and eternity. There is no other "last frontier." How much more could one achieve in the brief life one is given? That is the question Dante pursues in Paris. Or as Eliot put it six centuries later, pondering how to reach his Paradise: "How do we live in time to conquer time?"

*

THE BOAT THAT took the poet north is said to have docked briefly in Avignon in Provence. The site of the first love poets, the troubadours, and the earliest mystic Kabbalists, Avignon is now the seat of the church's power—wooed from *caput mundi* and held captive, Dante believed. The new pope had moved the papacy north that very year, 1309, impelled by the promise of vast riches. This was the beginning of the Babylonian Captivity, Clement V holding his court at Avignon and never setting foot in Italy. The church had become the richest banker in Europe by being the most aggressive tax collector. Dante calls the church "fuia"—a "thieving wench"—whom France, a "giant," will come to slay (*Purgatorio* 33.43–45). To support its building projects and its appetite for war, the church required massive streams of revenue, beyond what Italy's agrarian economy could provide. Avignon, the meeting point on the Rhône of half a dozen key alpine routes to the sea, was the source for extravagant tolls.

Were they both too late in their pilgrimages north, Dante and the pope? Paris was entering a period of misery, the first glimmerings of pestilence, famine and war that did not subside until the dawn of the Renaissance. Beginning in the early fourteenth century, a series of severe political, economic and natural crises hit northern Europe and drastically affected Parisian life. The rural sector stopped expanding. High population density and lack of new lands caused fragmentation into plots that could not support subsistence.

Landless peasants became day laborers to survive. The great monastic orders founded no new abbeys. The city smelled of smoke, hay, animals and burning flesh. King Philip the Fair began purging the glorious Right Bank temple of its Templars, whose trials and public burnings did not end until 1314 with the arrest of Grand Master Jacques du Molay. Soap only made conditions worse: its principal use was as an enema.

Dante's journey from Avignon wound through the land of ghosts. The tombs of Christian soldiers buried by the thousands in nearby Arles made the ground uneven. At the university, genius was more apparent among the dead than the living. Thomas Aquinas: dead and gone. Hugh of St. Victor, probably the greatest reader who ever lived, head of the Augustinian monastery of the Victorines: dead and gone. For Hugh, knowledge was not light as in the eighteenth-century notion of "the light of reason." He sought the light that brought man to a glow: the wisdom that makes the reader radiant. Dante wrote of Hugh's less magnificent brother Richard in *Paradiso* 10.132:

che a considerar fu più che viro

He whose meditation made him more than man

(trans. Mandelbaum)

Dead too: the theologian Bonaventure, and the Leonardo of the thirteenth century, Roger Bacon, author of a treatise on educational reform "which could have revived Medieval Christianity." Bacon was thrown into prison and died in 1292. Master of the sacred page Siger of Brabant had been stabbed to death by his demented secretary in 1284 for not recanting Aristotelianism with enough fervor. The secretary wanted a better denial of mortality, and found it in the stabbing. Dante awarded Siger immortality (10.137–38).

esse è luce etterna di Sigieri,
che, . . . silogizzò invidiosi veri.

it is the flame, eternally elated,
> of Siger . . . who syllogized truths for which he would
> be hated.

(trans. Ciardi)

One hungry ghost could not be denied: the Gothic. The great age of Gothic cathedral building was also over and with it the vast economic growth created in building these leviathans. But its impact was spreading. The last flying buttress of Notre Dame de Paris, whose foundation had been dedicated in 1163, was completed only a few years before Dante arrived, after two hundred years in the making. "Great buildings, like great mountains, are the work of centuries," Victor Hugo would write in the nineteenth century. Given that most people lived shoved together in dark, smoke-filled huts, the cathedrals were a magnificent spectacle. The Gothic was the portrait of the soul in the High Middle Ages: multiform, elaborate and ever rising. But for reasons of aesthetics, science and meditative rigor, the cathedrals could be created nowhere but in and around the earthly star, the six-pointed landscape of the Île de la Cité. With Paris at its center, the Île de France radiated to Chartres, Beauvais, Reims, Amiens, Bourges and Rouen, all cathedral cities.

The stones of Paris were the keepers of the last language Dante would teach himself to reach perfection. It was a language that united all the arts: music, architecture, poetry, vision. Light. Beatrice will instruct Dante how to see through mortal blindness, and to see through her smile to the meaning of love as the source of creativity. Dante will try to write what he sees.

★

THE MODERN WORLD with all its technological savvy can no longer build Gothic cathedrals, says the art historian Hans Jantzen. That is because we no longer understand them. But Dante did, and so we need to linger inside these masterpieces. The Gothic soul created works of enormous energy and improvisation, built with intricate complexity using the allegedly secret formulas of the Masons. As one looks at them or stands inside them, one's soul soars. One becomes what one beholds: a tree of a thousand branches, reaching upward to meet and embrace the sky. One discovers what had been incomprehensible to "the short wings of reason" which do not fly true, Dante will write in Canto 3 of *Paradiso*.

Dante had never seen a Gothic cathedral until Paris. The university was housed in Notre Dame. The cathedral at Siena is Romanesque with Gothic detailing. The church at Orvieto is transitionally Gothic. Both are restrained compared to French churches. Those differences would have struck Dante: the twelfth-century glassworker would sooner have worn a landscape on his back than have costumed his church with it. To such an artisan, the genius of Tuscany might appear shallow. The frescoes on the walls of Italian churches were painted to hide the deficiencies in the walls.

The paradise which the Gothic church reached for was the vision of a small abbot named Suger. His benefactor, Bernard of Clairvaux, liked to remind the abbot that he sucked at the breasts of wisdom. *Suger* means "to suck." To the diminutive Suger—who reduced others to mere specks inside his massive cathedrals—the image of himself as a suckling infant must have been as disquieting as was one observer's wonderment at how such a "weak little frame" could stand the strain of so "vigorous and lively a mind." More encouraging perhaps was Bernard's famous statement, "We are as dwarfs mounted on the shoulders of giants, so that we can perceive much more than they." Yet Suger knew how to manipulate this power-hungry ascetic. Bernard was the aspiring lord and master of western Europe. But Suger would let nothing come between himself and his own vision, which was to become the poet whose art transformed the onlooker from miles away—a text writ large. Suger's designs for cathedrals would change the face of Europe and the future of Europeans more indelibly than Bernard's war lust, his instigation of the terrible Crusades. Like Dante, Suger would seek out the coarsest, heaviest material, his "vulgar"—stone—to test his ability to express truth.

The monks of Suger's Saint-Denis ate bread "white as hail," and drank wines good enough to serve to God, they boasted. The abbot desired conviviality as much as Bernard distrusted it. As a "beggar lifted up from the dunghill," so he refers to his humble beginnings, he revels in his success. He sneaked precious gems into the church on the back of the Great Cross, a work he commissioned, a fan dance: on one side the suffering Savior; on the other, jewels of rose and agate and pearl and porphyry. Did he love God because the potentate was beauty? Or did he love beauty because it was a secondary revelation of God? Abelard was embarrassed by Suger, who wore the leftover jewels during mass and when he was tucking into a side of mutton. When Bernard finally saw one of Suger's decorating projects, he denounced it as "a workshop of Vulcan." Suger loved symbols of perfection. The baubles he received from visiting royalty delighted him, although he eventually offered them to the Holy Martyrs, a charitable order that converted pearls and gems into money for alms. When some exceptionally long beams were needed for a new western part of the cathedral at Saint-Denis, he wrote in the records of his administration, "I began to think in bed that I myself should go through all the forest in these parts." He was tireless in behalf of beauty.

Bernard was Suger's chief constraint. Bernard had pushed for new discipline and new churches, loathing religious painting done in the style that came to be known as Romanesque. Art was to be reduced to the essence. He wanted his churches simple, so that Christian souls might find grandeur within themselves. Bernard believed that illumination of the air—light—would convey the transcendent to the senses. On this, he and Suger agreed. In the manner and style of their goal to open a route to Paradise and deliver souls straight upward, they differed.

It was an eye-to-eye war that never erupted into a political battle, as most everything else at the time did. The two most ambitious men in France realized they could destroy each other or help each other. They both blinked. Suger worked behind the scenes to eliminate a friend of his, the only other cleric who stood a chance of being named counselor to the king. Stephen of Garlande was pushed or fell from power, leaving a vacuum for Bernard. In return, Suger got Bernard's support to rebuild the royal abbey of Saint-Denis just outside of Paris.

In older churches, the notion of "the City of God" emphasized "City." In Gothic cathedrals, the emphasis was on God. To defy material forms was Bernard's command. Under Suger's execution, stone became diaphanous. He worked with hundreds of builders, and under his direction, walls became weightless, towering but parchment-thin. The point was to give an impression of the ethereal. Even the sculptures carried out this theme: classical sculptures stand rooted to the earth. Gothic sculptures rise with the stone.

Suger got what he wanted: Elaborate stone structural systems and rose windows to a large degree replaced Byzantine mosaics and paintings as models for the earthly and the eternal. They were more than representations; they *were* heaven.

The genius of the cathedrals arises from the tension between these two social architects. The spires of Suger's cities of God are built on his model, intricate, highly ornamented, excessive, yet stunningly simple dramas of forked lightning or glittering icicles. As the famous nineteenth-century art historian John Ruskin noted: "No architecture is so haughty as that which is simple . . . the rude love of decorative accumulation: a magnificent enthusiasm which feels as if it could never do enough to reach the fullness of its ideal." The intent is to make the visitor imagine himself incarnated in God's will, a spiritual being who may suffer but will be redeemed. Gothic light is not natural but a reddish violet as filtered through the magnificent stained-glass windows, the light the fetus sees in the womb.

Even the Ravenna mosaics or Chinese porcelains are "dark" beside Suger's stained-glass windows, whose colors have never been reproduced. Some say it is the radiating power of the blue or the red. France had not had a single building of any note before Suger.

Suger's churches embodied the most important element Dante needed for Paradise. Not what they seemed, but what was hidden in their design. The reason the churches soared despite their weight and size were the methods that went beyond technique, that freed the artist to follow a greater inspiration, namely God the Creator. The churches seemed highly planned in their intricacy although they were improvisational in construction—there was no science of architecture at the time as we know it. Suger's methods of building went beyond technique. It is the illusion of delicacy—the height, thinner walls, and, often, the lack of interior columns—that the invention of buttresses made possible, that makes the viewer feel as if he is soaring upwards. The final, arching construct of Suger's grand vision contained not only the symbolism Dante will build into *Paradiso*—the vault of heaven or the speed of light through the stained-glass windows on which to ride upward past the blue sky—but also the instant inspirations the cathedral evokes.

> *e forse in tanto in quanto un quadrel posa*
> *e vola e da la noce si dischiava*

> *giunto mi vidi ove mirabil cosa*
> *mi torse il viso, a sé . . .*

> when—in the time it takes a bolt to strike,
> fly, and be resting in the bowstring's blur—

> I found myself in a place where a wondrous thing
> drew my entire attention. . . .

> (*Paradiso* 2.23–26; trans. Ciardi)

"Resting in the bowstring's blur" slows one's sense of time. But there is more: Dante embeds the secret of perfection in this image. He is looking at the arrow's flight from a perspective that bends time. *First* the bow hits the target, *next* it flies and *then* is released. Perhaps the better word is godlike: Dante's description begins with the end, with the purpose of the flight, the target.

Here was the final secret of how to defy one's medium. How to use language as Suger used stone: to create its opposite, which made it complete—all things, everything. In Suger's vision, stone's purpose, its perfection, is achieved when it become light and weightless. So in the highly decorated image-filled windows which Bernard disliked, the light transformed the image and the observer. To bend language so that it embodied not only the most ubiquitous, soulful speech of all, the vulgar, but to go further still, was Dante's challenge. For him that meant finding the language that was as rich and complete as silence. If Dante had any doubt that one could go beyond the human arts to achieve the unearthly—the eyes, the breath, the mind of God—he saw proof that it was possible in the stones of Paris.

*

THE SECRET LANGUAGE turned out to be numbers, sacred geometries, the science that allowed the ultrasecret Masons to realize their task—as they put it—"of raising a blessing from the ground," keeping the vision of a single building fresh for the hundred or two hundred years it took to complete the task. There were no tools of scale, which makes the achievement of cathedral-building even more astonishing. They were built on numeric harmonies.

The putative "secret" made the medieval Masons the intellectual fathers of America's Founding Fathers, who honored them by placing their symbols on the dollar bill, a symbol that empires can be built from grace and faith.

The "secret" by which Suger freed himself and his builders of tradition, of the lockstep of technique, was the square, the Pythagorean triangle, and the equilateral triangle—the "geometrical elite." These geometric figures were taught to painters and sculptors. These were the Masons' secrets: how to use these simple figures to enlarge a small sketch to the desired size of a finished work. "The equilateral triangle governed all decisive dimensions in the ground plans and elevations of the cathedrals of Chartres, Reims, Amiens, Cologne and Beauvais. None of these cathedrals was made with a drawing." Thus, in these buildings, despite their vastness and opulence of thought, "the element of Cistercian austerity is powerfully present." Some say that only these harmonies arouse the soul to listen or look in a way that makes a transformation possible. For Plato, goodness and beauty were in their deepest essence identical. For medieval architects, such mystic aesthetics had a "quieting and reassuring effect." The key figures were believed to be "the holy elements of which God himself had created the universe." The *Old Testament* says of God, "thou hast ordered all things in measure and number and weight" (Wisdom of Solomon 11:20). What were these numbers, and how did they help Dante in his most ambitious quest?

Eighty magnificent cathedrals were built in France between 1180 and 1270. They were the models for the *Comedy:* books in stone.

*

ON STRAW STREET, Dante sat among the students on bundles of fresh straw dropped on the cold stone floors, for there were no benches. Their long robes had flapped as they hurried through the Left Bank streets. Feet ground and shuffled in the dirty straw as the masters held forth on the nature of light and on the dark spots on the moon's surface and the errors creeping into the calendar through ignorance of astronomy. Astronomy, the mathematics of the stars, could "lift minds aloft, even unto the stars," as the ancient thinker Cassiodorus had suggested. Dante would have learned the state of the art of light in the new field of optics, which had begun in the mid-1200s. The marvel of curved mirrors began, and in their reflection, giants and dwarfs could change their shapes.

To our eyes, light is backdrop, "becoming material in all the diversity imposed upon it by the resistance of matter." How could Dante take in more light, which otherwise stopped here and there, at a book's surface, a tree, anything visible? Light had to mediate its strong energy, a scientist like Grosseteste believed, and so instead of light we had a visible—i.e., half in the dark—universe. There were three kinds of light: lux, lumen and splendor. Lux was light "in itself," light as the ubiquitous origin, from the sun. It penetrated to the very bowels of the earth to form minerals and sow the seeds of life. Lumen was the light that travels through space. Light which bounced off objects was called splendor, or color. Splendor was the light of Paradise.

*

THE VERY MODERN curriculum of the University of Paris was imbued with the teachings of the early Christian philosopher Boethius, who lived from 480 to 524. Dante had read Boethius's work *The Consolation of Philosophy* in Florence. Much of the prison imagery of *Inferno* is inspired by this work, which Boethius wrote while awaiting execution. In Paris, Dante would have had access to Boethius's more scholarly writings.

The last thing Boethius saw at the edge of his despair, beyond hope, beyond logic, looking only at sorrow and death as he lay dying in prison, falsely accused of betraying the king, Theodoric, was numbers. It was Suger's vision too, in his ecstasy. The one who had seen them first was Pythagoras, the ancient mathematician and magician. For Pythagoras, numbers had shapes: triangular numbers, square numbers, circular numbers. He discovered harmonic intervals and the triangle. "All things are numbers," he said. The whole of heaven was a musical scale. Appearances—devils and bedevilers of the soul—could be banished by an ability to see through the visible to the light, the splendor within, which took the form of numbers. Even in optimistic moments, Boethius's outlook was that of a sage concealing a distrust of the phenomenal world behind an admiration for "the beauty of mathematical noumena," Umberto Eco wrote. Math is a dogma that needs no verification.

Pythagoras saw the invisible noumena or spirits as numbers, beginning as the notion of opposites. The universe, he said, is made of men and women, the one and the many, light and darkness, rest and motion. All were in a constant state of addition and subtraction. Through their perception of numbers, Pythagoras and Boethius after him understood the properties of timeless moments. Pythagoras said that the most compelling forms are 1:2:4:8 and 1:3:9:27—"the same proportions that also determine the composition of the world soul." Art, music, human forms and ideas of state that are based on these proportions are the most pleasing and successful. The colossal cathedrals are built of music, notes and measures. Augustine, thinking of one man, one God, said the most admirable ratio is equality of symmetry, 1:1. Without the principle of Pythagorean order, Augustine says, the cosmos would return to chaos. Geometry leads the mind from the world of appearances to the contemplation of divine order.

One scholar counted sixty-seven pairs of eyes in *Inferno,* a testament to Dante's belief that we need to keep looking. To the eyes of "the last humanist," as Eco calls Boethius, the whole world is the work of a great architect, God. Architecture was frozen music, the music of the spheres. To know the order was to be overwhelmed by bliss. As Augustine wrote, "the most hidden things are the sweetest."

Boethius was, said Eco, a "sensitive intellectual in an age of profound crisis, an age occupied with the destruction of seemingly irreplaceable values. The classical world was vanishing before his eyes. It was a barbaric time. The cultivation of letters was dying out. The breakup of Europe had reached one of its most tragic moments. Boethius sought refuge by subscribing to values which could not be destroyed: the law of numbers, which would govern art and nature no matter what came to pass." Numbers alone were eternal, Boethius wrote. By meditating on numbers, one could free oneself of matter and appearances and learn directly from God.

Things could "radiate" the truth, wrote Bernard. They could "sound" the virtues. Anything beautiful involves the invisible becoming visible. "Even ugliness found a place, through proportion and contrast, in the harmony of things," writes Dantista Giuseppe Mazzotta. Evil itself became good and beautiful, for good was born from it and shone out more brightly by contrast. Geometry is the science of pure intellect and abstract vision. Vision is better than knowledge.

*

DANTE ASSIGNS EVERYTHING a place. The numbers in *Inferno, Purgatorio* and *Paradiso* are not random. The ten circles of Hell shift into the ten terraces of Mount Purgatory and the ten spheres of Heaven. The most discouraged lovers in Hell show up in Canto 5, because they have been duped by the five senses. We see not only Paolo and Francesca, the adulterous, punished lovers in *Inferno 5*; we are meant to see the full crimes of the five senses— "sensitive power without the rational." The evil King Nimrod utters five words in a line shortened to call attention to the number. But finally, up at the highest kingdom, lovers of God dwell in the five-petaled rose of Paradise. The recurrence in the *Commedia* of "nine" marks Dante's relationship with Beatrice, as we have seen. He meets her in the ninth hour of the ninth day of the ninth month of the year: she is his *omnia,* his everything, the trinity squared. The number of earthly aspirations is twelve. Nature moves in twelve months; a day is twelve hours. Twelve is the number of apostles. Noon has a special significance as representing celestial desire or divine eternity. Twelve is cyclical through time, though not perfectly circular. "The 'breath' is trinal, not triple." It is a tri-unity of three parts making a whole, not three things. Perhaps the most sacred number is ten. It represents the sum of the first four numbers $1 + 2 + 3 + 4$, depicted as a desire to rise: Four is the four corners of the world, three is the trinity, two is the soul yearning for an Other, and one is unity. The aesthetic of proportion was the medieval aesthetic par excellence.

Also Dante sees the world in rhyme that is deeper than appearance or simple soundalike rhythms. Three is unity of many in one, the trinity. Three trinities is the full light of grace. Threes expand into nines and then into twelves. He aims by use of numbers to collapse time into an eternal present: numbers unifying the essence of all the disparate-seeming events in a heightened, non-judgmental language of order. Dante would have known of Gregory the Great's "wild speculation"—John Donne called it in the seventeenth century—that "Unity is the beginning of number, as God is the beginning of thought." The language Dante is after is unity of multiplicity. Mandelstam marvels at Dante's "marriageable" endings. "It is as if all his words rhyme making one sound."

One might see Dante's consummate challenge as that of turning four into three. The entire journey and all of Paradise culminates in the image of a book: *quaderno*—a folded folio which is a medieval quarto or "volume." How does four—the book—become three, or God? The answer is by the principle of addition—of achieving unity in multiplicity. They come together in love. Or, less mystically, four becomes three by pointing out that it is not three—pointing, in other words, to something beyond itself. This is what the Gothic did so well: achieve unity out of multiplicity. As Virgil explains to Dante in *Purgatorio* 18.49–60, understanding comes mysteriously, like the green leaves from a plant:

> *Ogne forma sustanzïal, che setta*
> *è da matera ed è con lei unita,*
> *specifica vertute has in sé colleta,*
>
> *la qual sanza operar non è sentita,*
> *ne si dimonstra mai che per effetto,*
> *come per verdi fronde in pianta vita.*
>
> *Però, là onde vegan lo 'ntelleto*
> *de le prime notizie, omo non sape,*
> *e de' primi appetibili l'affetto,*

che sono in voi sì come studio in ape
  di far lo mele; e questa prima voglia
  merto di lode o di biasmo non cape.

Every substantial form, which is at once
  distinct from matter and united with it,
  has a specific virtue stored within it

known only by its operation
  and revealed by the effect it has,
  as the green leaves reveal the life of a plant.

And so, nobody knows where they come from,
  the understanding of the first ideas,
  or the fondness for the first object of passion;

they are in you, as the need to make honey
  is in the bee, and for this primary
  urge there is no place either for praise or blame.

(trans. Merwin)

★

TO THE POET, this was the next-to-last leap: the idea that there could be a perfect page, a page that needed nothing more. Logical impossibilities make the best realities, like organizations that have no center, but are centers everywhere (as is the case in the air traffic control system). When Dante looked back on his life, the days and experiences seemed many and chaotic. How to explain that a chance encounter of a young man and a girl in medieval Florence could at the same time contain within it the pattern of universal salvation—Dante's journey from Beatrice's city of Florence to a hellish slave-culture like that of Egypt, then to a lost Eden suggesting Jerusalem, and then to a just and timeless heavenly city prefiguring the possibility of a renewed Rome? He needed to give a shape of significance to his whole life, not the ready made victim-martyr formula the law of Florence and Boniface had imposed upon him. He saw himself less and less in these years as a political target and more as a chosen being, like the Jews who fled Pharaoh's slavery, wandered the desert and were saved by loving God. He could tell this story by seeing the events in the same way the stones of Paris told transcendent stories: through the holy numbers that are in themselves emblems of the story of his ascent.

Language alone cannot do that. This is not a medieval view. The modern philosopher and deconstructionist Jacques Derrida says, if it's written, it's dead. Writing captures only what has happened, not the eternal unfolding present in which the reader can experience exactly what the author experienced. Dante goes to the edge of language and vision, the numbers he hopes will keep him from slipping into the unreadable when he flirts with the still, silent center of Paradise, where nothing is desired, not the past, not words, nor ego, where restlessness has ended. In Paradise, he will say, the imperfection makes it possible to see the perfection. Writing is the shadow. Dante, in "a new vision," will read the truthful thought behind faces as if written in a book:

Quali per vetri trasparenti e tersi,
  o ver per acque nitide e tranquille,
    non sì profonde che i fondi sien persi,

tornan d'i nostri visi le postille
   debili sì, che perla in bianca fronte
   non vien men forte a le nostre pupille . . .

As in clear glass when it is polished bright,
   or in a still and limpid pool whose waters
   are not so deep that the bottom is lost from sight,

a footnote of our lineaments will show,
   so pallid that our pupils could as soon
   make out a pearl upon a milk-white brow . . .

                    (*Paradiso* 3.10–15; trans. Ciardi)

Paradise is structured as a hierarchy of shadows. Meaning only comes through differentiation, what mystics call the *via negativa*. One can talk about God only in paradoxes—a circle whose center is everywhere and circumference nowhere. God can be described—in our speech—only by what He is not.

The world is a book; God is its author. What makes *Paradiso* so difficult is that it is dedicated to its own impossibility. Language is forced to reveal its shortcomings. Dante uses the image of white on white: a pearl on a milk-white brow. A shadow of a shadow. Paradisical reality can be intuited; it cannot be conveyed. That is what makes *Paradiso* the most modern part of the *Commedia:* the poetry of its own ineffability. It is the drama of transcendence: to be drawn inside-out in order to reach *libertà,* liberty, a state of grace.

The nineteenth-century German composer Robert Schumann wrote a piece of music as a love letter to his wife Clara. On the top of the score of the last movement, he scribbled a quotation from the philosopher and Dantista Friedrich Schlegel: "Through all the notes in earth's multi-colored dream, there sounds one soft long-drawn note for the one who listens in secret." In the last note of the final movement, the pianist is instructed to hold down the four-note C major chord until well after it melts into silence. That silent note is the most memorable in the entire heartbreakingly beautiful piece, the most eternal. Dante writes around 1317, perhaps as early as the first canto of *Paradiso* was written: "We are given to understand by the apostle [Paul] speaking *ad Corinthios,* where he says, 'I know such a man (whether in the body or out of the body I know not, God knoweth), who was rapt in the third heaven [Paradise], and heard hidden words.' "

"When you finally manage to utter what you wish to utter, the rest is silence." Dante had perceived the vibrant language of silence. He had read it in stone. To write it was his next challenge.

*

> . . . *ché ciò procede*
> *da perfetto veder, che, come apprende,*
> *così nel bene appreso move il piede.*

> [It's] perfected vision that sees the good
> and step by step moves nearer to what it sees.

(*Paradiso* 5.5–6; trans. Ciardi)

Perhaps Dante knew he was flirting with the limitations of poetry and form, flirting with madness, in Paris in 1309 or so. The time wasn't yet right for the leap into Paradise. He pulled back. In 1311, the news must have reached him in Paris that Henry VII was crossing the Alps on his way to Italy. Dante had to be there to offer advice and support. It is believed that by mid-December Dante too crossed the Alps. He knelt before Henry and pledged his loyalty: "I who set down this letter as much for myself as for others saw and heard in you all that imperial majesty should be: the utmost in loving kindness and mercy. I saw this when my hands were placed in yours and my lips paid their debt of homage."

Only in Italy will the last barrier be broken and the sunlight melt the ice in his soul. He will finish *Purgatorio* around 1312 with fresh ideas for where the journey would end when in 1316 he finally began *Paradiso*.

Dantean Journeys

Dante called architecture—and clothing—"the mother arts." They contain the body as the body contains the soul. Over both they exert the strongest but subtlest form of authority. The most ambitious students of Paradise have been the social architects who build the promise of "a perfect place" in the imagery of despotism.

The Brownshirts, servitors of the Third Reich, corrupt Dantisti, plundered the High Middle Ages for their dangerous utopian symbols. Third Reich means "Third Empire," the medieval state of Paradise. Fascists have drawn on theories of harmony and an ideal life operating in *Paradiso* to wield a governing influence on people's souls. Fascism is Italian, suggesting community in the medieval sense, agrarian and feudal. An architect, Giuseppe Terragni, steeped in Italian fascism, designed a building he called the

Danteum, "to carry out the celebration of Dante's words as a primary source for Mussolini's creations." Il Duce fell in love with the plans. The idea was to reconstruct the pilgrim's journey through a long entrance beginning in a forest of one hundred columns, through a serpentine walk past a series of sculptures writhing in agony, then into a new image of the universal Roman Empire and intense sunlight in a square of the courtyard. "The reconstruction of a space in which to live a miraculous adventure would, it was assumed, attract hundreds of thousands of pilgrims to emerge from stone and sculpture into a blinding light and become pure— the men and women of paradise.

"The adventure is that 'higher aesthetic value,' and can be reached only through formal and logical relationships that one can build following an abstract and nearly invisible trace." The plans for the unbuilt building might have been destroyed: Allies bombed Terragni's studio in 1944, but his partner had carried home the drawings the night before. The Danteum might well have been built "had the war not occurred."

The great Nijinsky said when asked to explain his famous leaps, "I just forget to come down." Paradise is a compelling height, and a dangerous one. Those who take the language of perfection seriously believe in order and strict controls, but they miss Dante's love of freedom. Paradise defines human perfection as the art of pleasure where all desire is ended. The quest for Dantisti lies in how to distinguish paradises that are false. That was Dante's last important quest.

CHAPTER 9

"We Have Tears for Things," Said Virgil

THE LAST TIME DANTE, NOW FORTY-SIX, HAD BEEN IN THE Casentino region, he was twenty-four years old, a soldier fighting in the famous Battle of Campaldino, a bloody victory for the Guelfs' control of Florence in the endless battle against the Ghibellines. His side celebrated victory by dressing donkeys in pope's mitres and throwing them over the city walls to show their contempt for the slain archbishop. Casentino had been laid waste many times by the factional fighting. The upper Arno valley, beautiful and wild, was dominated by castles; the mountains alone could not provide sufficient protection for the medieval lords. Climbing these hills today, one edges along tree lines where ibexes still saunter at dawn and dusk. This was the place to see flocks of golden eagles that looked like huge embers of the sun pouring down from the sky. In summer, scads of butterflies stick to the droplets on a swimmer's skin. This is Italian resort country now, consecrated not to battles but to sparkling Asti wines. Dante believed it possible to see from here a star Adam would have seen from Paradise.

What Dante saw unfold from these heights as he struggled to complete the middle canticle of his own passage to freedom, *Purgatorio*, was the descent of the presumed political savior Henry VII of Luxembourg into Italy. Returning to Italy to come to his aid,

Dante wrote him on the nature of Florentine politics: "Florence," he warns, "is an asp that bites its own mother's womb." He advises Henry on how he might unify Italy's deadly factions. The year after Henry's death, Dante will write *De Monarchia (On Monarchy)*, his treatise on how people should live together. He has given up fighting for any man; now he fights only for an idea—the need to bridge the gap between poetry and politics, the desires of the soul and the ideals of empire. He is writing two *Purgatorio*s at the same time: *De Monarchia* will enrage many. It will be burnt in 1329, eight years after his death. In 1554, it will be placed on the Vatican's Index of Banned Books, removed only in 1886.

But the cruelest moment in literature, said Byron, is when Virgil is dismissed from the *Comedy*. Virgil is Dante's master, his guide, his sweet father, the poet who has raised his ambitions from love lyrics to epics, and his departure is for many readers the crashing end of the *Comedy*. Who wants to continue on to a paradise that would not admit such a great soul, such a guide?

As Dante climbs Mount Purgatorio, he walks to the right of Virgil, as he followed him on the left side down into Hell. Walk on the right side. The pun in his step tells us he is righting himself. It is a calculated risk for Dante to lose a beloved character.

Publius Virgilius Maro—Virgil—is assigned to Limbo, the air-conditioned chamber of Hell which other poets inhabit, deprived of light; and Virgil defines his whole existence as "suspicion." Beatrice steps into this gloom and, astonishingly, Virgil recognizes her. He believes she is Lady Philosophy. She had addressed him in *Inferno* 2 with the respect the great poet deserves, and asked him to lead her cowering lover from the dark wood to her at the top of Purgatory, where she will guide him the rest of the way to Paradise. When Virgil tells Dante all this in *Inferno*, Dante understands that he is one of the elect, chosen for a great fate, but for the next sixty cantos, he hangs on to Virgil for dear life:

. . . ch'un sol volere e d'ambedue:
tu duca, tu segnore e tu masetro

My Guide! My Lord! My master! Now lead on:
one will shall serve the two of us in this.

(*Inferno* 2.133–35; trans. Ciardi)

Virgil accepts this assignment knowing how difficult the trip will be. To move toward the light, Dante will have to confront everything that is murky and tangled not only in himself but within all of humanity. He knows because he has led his own hero, Aeneas, through the underworld. Aeneas, the mythical thirteenth-century B.C. founder of the Roman people. But Dante is unlike Aeneas. Dante is curious about everything, always stopping to question the souls. He is, after all, living life as a comedy and so he can afford to seem ignorant, unlike Virgil who sees life as a tragedy. It is a new quality in heroes, this joyous ignorance. At every step, Virgil has to challenge Dante, even teach him the manners of the afterlife, such as how to hug a vaporous shade so his arms don't end up in self-embrace, or how to manage his mortal weight to keep from sinking Charon's boat when they sail to the Inferno. Virgil's seductive words finesse them out of impossible situations. Virgil cleanses the dirt of Hell from Dante's face so this mortal being does not attract suspicion as an interloper, like a wall casting a shadow, among these ethereal creatures.

"Explain love to me," Dante demands of Virgil in *Purgatorio* after all the guide's exertions. Virgil says, "I have demonstrated it."

Dimonstri. He patiently listens as Dante insolently compares him to a loser in a game of dice (*Purgatorio* 6). He shows no reaction to hearing Dante snicker when the great Roman poet Statius declares himself saved by the *Aeneid* (*Purgatorio* 22).

As they climb, Virgil's powers decline and he begins to lose his way. He sees things he has never seen before. In *Purgatorio* 29.52–57, Dante notices seven trees turn into seven candelabra flaming "more radiantly than the mid-month moon shines at midnight in an untroubled sky" (Mandelbaum trans.). Dante looks to Virgil for an answer, but he is met with silence. And then, at the height of his labors, the selfless guide is sent back to Limbo. He has come within reach of a Paradise he will never enjoy. This "loftiest poet" born seventy years before Christ, who read the fortunes of emperors and made their wives weep with his words, has been sweet sanity itself.

Mark Twain in *Pudd'nhead Wilson* says that if a character gets in the way, just have him walk into the backyard and fall down a well. Aristotle has cautioned against eliminating a beloved figure: the killing off of a great character at the end of Act 2 makes it likely that the audience will spend Act 3 somewhere else. Nahum Tate rewrote *King Lear* in the eighteenth century to spare Cordelia because Shakespeare's audiences were enraged by her death.

Dante prepares himself to lose everything that is unessential, everything he hopes for. This is how, finally, he becomes a poet, not as a hero by exalting himself with great deeds, but by going in the opposite direction: eliminating everything but what helps him transcend his sorrows. In *Inferno*, Dante learned what makes sin so attractive. Can one turn away? One can, if one believes in will and control; these are the keys to *Purgatorio*. Lust, power, passion: the souls in Hell gave in to these thrills, but their pleasure was transient. Throughout *Purgatorio,* the question is posed: Does one make real choices, or do desires overpower the aim to be excellent? We are responsible for the choices we make. What we choose, invariably, is what we love. Dante's education consists of seeing the misery of being in love with the things that fade—sex, money, prestige—and directing his will to choose what is immortal, God, or perfection. One cannot see God if one is interested in something else.

*

DANTE AND VIRGIL notice along the mountain terraces a number of works of art. The art is even better than the art of nature. The portraits are so vivid they seem to speak. In life, one moves around a sculpture; here the sculptures move around the souls. This is art crafted with God's hand. It is like Giotto's advances in realism, his paintings of saints that vie with the real saints. It is an affirmation too of Dante's own uniquely realistic art. Along these terraces the poets make their way, encountering souls bent over carrying heavy stones on their backs. They are forced to move slowly and to concentrate on the art under foot and on the mountainsides. The souls consider themselves God's art.

Purgatory is process-oriented. Hell and Heaven are eternal places, but Purgatory is a passage, the link between the butterfly's wings. Purgatory is dominated by time, change, and hope. The souls here have been given temporal sentences. They are working toward freedom from pride, avarice, envy, anger, gluttony, sloth and lust. There is day and night. In Hell, there is only dark, and in Paradise there is only daylight. Every soul who enters Purgatory will go on to Paradise eventually, and they know this. Though the stones they bear are heavy, the goal is present.

Man writes in crooked lines, Dante says, noting that God writes in straight lines. He is challenged to go beyond craft, cut off the last "guide," his beloved father-poet, and learn to read a deeper message. Can he read the writing on the surface of the sea, or in the order of human relations? Can he decode the mysteries of goodness hidden inside evil?

★

THINK OF DANTE without Virgil; think of Beethoven losing his hearing in 1804 at the age of thirty-four. The loss enabled Beethoven to experiment free from the intrusive sounds of the external environment; free from the rigidities of the material world; free to combine and recombine the stuff of reality in accordance with his desires, into previously undreamed of forms and structure. Perhaps this is why Beethoven accepts his loss. And it is why, ultimately, Dante acquiesces to his greatest loss, the loss of faith in poetry itself.

There is a moment in one's reading of Dante, says the critic Clive James, when one realizes that all one has learned to enjoy in poetry is everything that Dante outgrew. Since 1302, Dante has been systematically renouncing the thrill of art. But between the years 1308 and 1312—the *Purgatorio* years—he engages in a deliberate program of weaning himself from his craft and letting go of its dazzle.

"For a poet to lose such a talent would have been a misfortune," says James. "For a poet to give it up was an act of disciplined renunciation rarely heard of." Poetry saved Dante. Virgil saved

Dante. But then what? Saved for what? Dante boasts that he knows Virgil's epic, begun in 26 B.C., *"tutta quanta"*—"all of it by heart" (*Inferno* 20.114). But there is a vast difference between the two: Within the *Commedia*, Virgil was destined to go to Hell. Dante had a choice whether or not to go. Virgil did not. If Virgil cannot get into Paradise, it suggests that not every mortal can attain divine grace. But if Beatrice can get in, if Guido Guinizelli and a host of forgotten poets can get close enough, then why not him? For that matter, why not us? Too often, the reason is self-absorption.

No wonder that Byron, self-invented down to his fake military uniform, which he wore to charm Venetian society, lamented Virgil's disappearance. The end of art could, for the artist, be the end of life. For Dante, it is the beginning of something new.

*

THE YEARS 1311–12 were full of hopes. The hopes were aroused by young King Henry, who had ruled tiny Luxembourg ably and, when the German king Albert I died, was elected to the vacant throne. His ambition was to conquer the Holy Land and unite Germany and Italy. When word spread of his intentions, he was welcomed to Italy by those who were eager to overthrow papal greed. The popes, intent on keeping Italy divided, had for years managed to keep the Holy Roman Emperor out. Roman law was one of the glories of the world, yet the aggression of the popes and the reluctance of the emperors to challenge them reduced Italy to chaos. It was Henry's plan to take the safest, not the most direct, route from Lombardy through Forlì. For at least six months in the late winter and early spring, summer and perhaps early autumn, armies were growing both in support of Henry and against him. There were revolts throughout Tuscany, but Henry had his 6,000 knights, more than 2,000 of them Italians. There was reason to be encouraged.

But Brescia, the first city to be fought over, did not crumple as expected. The gold-rich Florentine coffers supplied opposition towns with bread and credit. Henry's supporter, the cardinal of Prato, fretted, "What colossal impudence, these Florentines. With ten louse eggs"—a reference to the florins, which bore some resemblance to larvae—"they will try anything." By comparison to the Florentines, Henry was poor, and he taxed the towns he entered in order to feed his soldiers. The taxes transformed supporters into enemies.

And then Henry received an offer that seemed certain to change his fortunes. Pope Clement promised to move up his coronation as Holy Roman Emperor if he arranged a marriage between his daughter and the eldest son of King Robert of Naples. Certain that this would advance his cause, Henry delayed his march to set these plans in motion. Dante must have suspected that Clement had offered Henry a dull weapon, and the king had taken it. The Florentines took advantage of the delay to stir up opposition to Henry.

At this same time, Dante's appeal had finally come before the Florentine fathers. They refused to annul his sentence and allow him to return home. Finally, Henry pushed on with his campaign. Battles ensued; there were some successes, but many failures. In Rome, he could not even subdue the street fighting. Then, in 1312, Henry laid siege to Florence and his luck ran out. After a bad winter, he fell ill and died. His death is variously attributed to dysentery or to a Dominican friar poisoning the sacramental wine. "This," said one historian, "is how Italy repays her importunate lovers."

As Henry met his fate, Dante was probably climbing Falterona, forty-two miles east of Florence. A visitor could see the whole of Tuscany from this height of 5,140 feet, the highest peak in this part of the Apennines, and would recognize what Dante must have seen: that it is shaped like a heart, although a badly drawn one.

Henry's empty chair is Dante's last sight of him in *Paradiso*. Instead of hopes for a golden age, there is confusion and disaster. In the absence of justice, Augustine said, all that is left is for men and women to keep from doing evil. No more can be expected.

*

IT STANDS TO reason that Dante knew all along that at some point he would have to drop Virgil down a well. Virgil offers to disappear as early as *Inferno* 1.121–23: ". . . a soul more worthy than I am will guide you." Dante had come to believe that one risked more with a guide than alone. To the medieval imagination, Virgil was an unconsecrated saint. He was presumed to be not just a poet, but a prophet. He was thought to have predicted the coming of Christ in his fourth eclogue. He was writing about the son of a Roman consul—Pollio—but the medievals insisted that he saw Jesus forty years before his birth. Legends maintained that Virgil erected an invisible bubble over Florence that kept out the mosquitoes, and that he threw a golden leech into the Arno that made fish fat.

*

FIRE. THE STORY is told that when Virgil was completing the *Aeneid*, which he had spent eleven years writing, he became gravely ill, that he lingered for several days in a fever and then, summoning some strength, got up from his bed, gathered the pages of his unfinished manuscript, and threw them into the fire. The emperor Augustus, who had commissioned him to write the poem in honor of himself and his deeds, had feared such an outcome and had stationed a guard at the poet's bedside. Augustus knew that deeds are forgotten unless a poet records them. The guard put his hand in the fire and recovered the singed pages. Virgil's incomplete manuscript would be published upon his death and against his dying wishes, made to his friends, Varius and Tucca, to burn the pages the emperor saved.

Virgil wrestled with fears of creative impotence. His biographer, Donatus, wrote that he used to dictate lines of his poetry in the mornings and then spend the whole day working them over: "He produced his poetry as a she-bear does her cubs: licking it gradually into shape." John Milton formulated the lines of *Paradise Lost* at night, while others slept. When his daughters arrived in the morning, he would dictate the lines, saying as he did so that he felt like a cow being milked. Two men, writing of empire and emotion, both imagining themselves an inspiring likeness to female animals. Dante turned it inside out: Beatrice, the woman of shining genius, will pull his very best work from him.

In the final test through which Virgil leads Dante, there is again the poet's fire. The two are nearly within sight of the earthly Paradise, the summit of the Purgatorial Mountain, in Canto 27. Virgil urges Dante to walk through fire that stands between him and

Paradise. Dante has cowered before but never like this. He has fled
the fire: the Florentine charge hanging over his head is that he be
burned at the stake if he should be seized. He has seen souls burn
in Hell. From inside a purgatorial flame, he hears the voice of
Arnaut Daniel, a gambler, an impoverished aristocrat who
became a troubadour. Arnaut wrote the lost epic *Lancelot* which
had so stirred *Inferno*'s Paolo and Francesca that they committed
adultery. The adulterers wind up in Hell, but the poet winds up in
Purgatory, destined to reach Paradise. Arnaut had the right
instincts but the wrong reactions. He dedicated himself to love,
which was good, but recklessly, which was bad. In a poem, he con-
fesses.

I never had her, but she has me
Forever in her power—Love . . .

. . . I am Arnaut, who hoards the wind
And chases the rabbit with the ox
And swims against the swelling tide.

Dante greets Arnaut as the "finest craftsman of words," bend-
ing language to the breaking point. When the ballad form proved
too simple for the visions in his head, Arnaut had created new
forms. One was the sestina, a song so intricately rhymed that it
makes everything unrhymed sound unfinished. Arnaut has spent
one hundred years in this flame, sobering up from the excesses of
"my old folly" as he prepares himself for Paradise. When he fin-
ishes talking to Dante,

Poi s'ascose nel foco che li affina.

Then he hid himself in the fire that refines them.

(*Purgatorio* 26.148; trans. Merwin)

Look toward me, says Virgil. Come to me and free yourself of last fear: the refining fire.

"*Più non si va, se pria non morde,*
anime sante, il foco: intrate in esso,
e al cantar di là non siate sorde"

. . . "There is no going past here without
the bite of fire first. . . . Enter it
without being deaf to the singing beyond it"

(27.10–12; trans. Merwin)

One of the angels of God says this to Dante, and Virgil comforts him.

"*Figliuol mio,*
qui puo esser tormento, ma non morte."

"There may be
torment here, my son, but not death."

(27.20–21; trans. Merwin)

"On the other side, Beatrice waits," Virgil promises Dante. On the other side is the freedom of the true dreamer to combine and recombine the stuff of reality according to one's true desire. He is crossing a divide between poetry, politics and philosophy to what the medievals called grace. Dante goes into the flame.

In *Inferno,* Dante watched Ulysses being consumed by the flame, but the flame did not consume him. On the mountain, Dante undergoes the same purgations as the souls he encounters. No longer the detached observer, he is now the participant. "Dante's is the parable of an author writing a book or creating a masterpiece, educating himself along the way, acknowledging the two are mirror images—the more beautiful the maker, the sweeter the work," famed Dantista Leo Spitzer wrote in the twentieth century.

Commentators debate whether Virgil also walks through the fire which, he promised Dante, would not harm a hair on his head, even if he stayed in it for a hundred years. He greets Dante on the other side:

> "*Il temporal foco e l'etterno*
> *venduto hai, figlio; e se' venuto in parte*
> *dov'io per me più oltre non discerno. . . .*"

> "You have seen the temporal fire
> and the eternal, my son, and you have come
> to where I, by myself, can see no farther."

> (27.127–29; trans. Merwin)

And then Virgil says farewell:

> *"Non aspettar mio dir più né mio cenno;*
> *libero, dritto e sano è tuo arbitrio,*
> *e fallo fora non fare a suo senno:*
>
> > *per ch'io te sovra te corono e mitrio."*

"Expect no further word or sign from me.
Your own will is whole, upright, and free,
and it would be wrong not to do as it bids you,

> therefore I crown and mitre you over yourself."
>
> > (27.139–42; trans. Merwin)

The need for justice gives way to Dante's achievement. The crown that Henry was promised, Dante gets to wear as he becomes emperor of himself.

> *volsimi a la sinistra col respitto*
> *col quale il fantolin corre a la mamma*
> *quando ha paura o quando elli è afflitto,*
>
> > *per dicere a Virgilio: "Men che dramma*
> > *di sangue m'è rimaso che non tremi:*
> > *conosco i segni de l'antica fiamma."*

> I turned to the left with the confidence that
> a little child shows, running to its mother
> when something has frightened or troubled it,

to say to Virgil, "Not even one drop
of blood is left in me that is not trembling;
I recognize the signs of the old burning."

(30.43–48; trans. Merwin)

"*Conosco i segni de l'antica fiamma,*" Dante says, quoting a line from
the *Aeneid* that Dido speaks, recognizing she is falling in love with
Aeneas, having felt no such stirrings since her husband died. The
love, *antica fiamma,* pulses through Dante's veins for Virgil and for
Beatrice.

Ma Virgilio n'avea lasciati scemi
di sé, Virgilio dolcissimo patre,
Virgilio a cui per mia salute die'mi;

né quantunque perdeo l'antica matre,
valse a le guance nette di rugiada
che, lagrimando, non tornasser atre.

But Virgil had left us, he was no longer there
among us, Virgil, most tender father,
Virgil to whom I gave myself to save me,

nor did all that our ancient parent
had lost have any power to prevent
my dew-washed cheeks from running dark with tears.

(30.49–54; trans. Merwin)

Even in his own poem, the *Aeneid,* Virgil doesn't reach bliss.
The souls he envisions go through purgation and then back into

their bodies. Aeneas, in Hell, asks his dead father why the souls pray for rebirth. Who would choose suffering again, even in "their mad longing for the light?" (*Aeneid* 6.719–21) His father offers no convincing answer.

As Virgil recedes from the *Commedia*, Dante is born. Only then does Beatrice appear and speak his name—Dante—the only time Dante is named in the poem. She says, scolding:

> "*Dante, perché Virgilio se ne vada,*
> *non pianger anco, non piangere ancora;*
> *ché pianger ti conven per altra spada.*"

> "Dante, though Virgil's leaving you, do not
> yet weep, do not weep yet; you'll need your tears
> for what another sword must yet inflict."

(30.55–57; trans. Mandelbaum)

Another sword? Beatrice makes him weep for failing her, for the distractions that he put between them.

Dante's tears for Virgil are his homage. Within ten lines, a sacred number, he cries Virgil's name out five times. Dante, do not weep, do not weep, do not weep. Each *pianger* is a sound of Beatrice's rebuke, catching him up in a way patient Virgil never had. Beatrice calls him to a higher vision of himself. She doesn't care that Dante has traveled through Hell and Purgatory to find her. Do not weep for Virgil, she says; think of how I died. For that you should cry. You loved me when I was a beautiful young woman, and now I am dust. But my body was always dust. Am I not more beautiful now that you can see my soul, which will never die? You did not worship my

soul when you were writing love poems. You did not see the value
I had for you. Do not confuse eternal beauty with common things.

Beatrice is echoing Virgil's own *Georgica, Book 4* (525–27), where
Orpheus's voice, calling the lost Eurydice, repeats her name down
the stream three times. Eurydice treads on a serpent. She is bitten
and dies. Her lover, the poet Orpheus, goes down to the underworld to bring her back. But though Orpheus can seduce Hades
into agreeing to his request, the god of the underworld adds one
condition: if Orpheus turns, Eurydice will vanish for good. At the
top of the underworld, almost free, Orpheus turns around before
they reach the upper levels, and she vanishes. Virgil's Orpheus
turns repetitions of the three *E*'s of Eurydice's name into the per-
sistent echo of weeping.

Three times Beatrice tells Dante not to weep. Each repetition
suggests Dante's faith that God is paying attention to his poem.
For the same reasons, the architects of Notre Dame de Paris put
gargoyles at the top of the towers. Not visible from below, this art
is meant for God's eye.

Dante. His name spoken by Beatrice, and he remembers who he
is. He is Dante. Unlike Virgil, Dante has refused to accept the
finality of death. He has recovered his lost soul, and here is Beatrice, brought back to life. Are they two distinct figures, or one—a
man looking at his soul as his equal? This may be the image of
love he has sought: the movements of the soul, obscure, mysterious, now standing before him. Beatrice: blessings. Augustine had
written that there are only two loves possible for man—the love of
self combined with the love of God—and at some point Dante
realizes they are one and the same.

As the Jews did for Augustine, who relied on the sacred nature of their holy texts, so Virgil carried the light for Dante and illumined the path behind him while he stumbled forward in the gloom. To Dante's eyes, Virgil made one mistake in life: he gave way to sorrow. Melancholy stands in the way of love's transforming pleasures. It is Virgil's tragedy. It is why he can save Dante, he can save Statius, but he cannot save himself.

> "... *Facesti come quei che va di notte,*
>   *che porta il lume dietro e sé non giova,*
>   *ma dopo sé fa le persone dotte* ..."

> "Like a night walker thou, who onward lies
>   bearing a light behind him, useless (true)
>   to himself, but making those who follow wise. ..."

> (*Purgatorio* 22.67–69)

This translation is Lawrence Binyon's, worked on in collaboration with Ezra Pound. It is known as the madman's Dante, a channeled voice, because Binyon wrote and Pound edited as they believed Dante would have spoken English. Merwin gives another perspective on this critical and moving event. Statius tells Virgil:

> "You first showed me the way
> to Parnassus to drink from its grottoes,
> and it was you, after God, who first enlightened me.

> You did what someone does walking at night
> holding the lantern behind him so that
> it does him no good but makes wise those who follow."

> (22.64–69)

This is the ultimate lesson drawn from Virgil's example. Even more than following the master poet's words, it is clear to Dante that love draws out Virgil's fear: love of a God he is not sure exists, or if he exists cannot return his love, even though that God may seem to answer his prayers. *"Di, si qua est coelo pietas, quae talia curet"*—"Gods, if there is some piety in heaven which cares for such things . . ." There is an emptiness in art. Aeneas saw it. Dante means to see through it as he meets Beatrice again and knows the greater mystery of grace:

> ". . . . there are tears for things; here too,
>   things mortal touch the mind. Forget your fears;
>   this fame will bring you some deliverance."
> He speaks. With many tears and sighs he feeds
> his soul on what is nothing but a picture."
>
> (*Aeneid* 1.655–59; trans. Mandelbaum)

Did Dante need Virgil as his guide? Beatrice could have asked Aristotle for that favor. But perhaps he would rather have put his arm around a tree. Aristotle's writings are forbidding. The awakening to Aristotle in the thirteenth century was the work of generations and took place in the cool light of intellectual research. The awakening of Virgil by Dante is an arc of flame which leaps from one great soul to the another. Virgil may have needed an arm around his shoulder. He defines his whole existence as suspension. "Without hope we live in desire." It's the only punishment Virgil undergoes.

★

WE CAN EXPECT no more from Dante than Dante expected from Virgil. He clears our path. The difference between them, ultimately, is the difference between Christian and Ancient views. Virgil is the poet of death: "I sing of warfare and the man," he begins the *Aeneid*. At the end, Aeneas is standing over his enemy, who begs for his life in the name of filial piety. Aeneas sees the buckle Turnus has taken from his own friend and is enraged. He plunges his sword into Turnus, whose soul rages from him. Aeneas does everything for piety and duty; he has been able to conquer everything but blood lust. We see the defeat of faith by death and also of love by death, as in the suicide of Dido, the queen Aeneas must reject because love will deter him from his life's work, the founding of Rome.

*

HOW MANY PAIRS of sandals has Dante worn out climbing these goat paths of Italy? The end of *Purgatorio* is the end of the road, but the true task is ahead. The real challenge for mythic heroes is not slaying the enemy or freeing the oppressed. It is in telling the story to those who have never seen a dragon.

Dantean Journeys

There is a force like a dragon in John Freccero, who has been teaching the *Comedy* for decades, currently at New York University. He walks into a classroom, rarely opens a book, and after two hours of lecturing flawlessly and without interruption, he leaves his listeners at the threshold of Paradise. Not one student has thought in those two hours about his plans for the weekend. He can unearth the thinking Dante may have undergone, making each word as encompassing as a world itself.

"*Vago* is the first word Dante the poet utters when he is on his own. It is a word full of pleasure. It suggests velleity, wind, motion, yearning, desire. Dante moves forward, letting pleasure be his guide now." The breezes grow soft, Dante moves *lento, lento,* after hurrying up the mountain. *Vago.* We are meant to taste the salty breeze and relax in Dante's long vowels. The god Aeolus keeps the precious winds for sailing locked in a mountain. They are jewels, worth a fortune to travelers. He releases them only as he pleases. "*Vago* is a word that loses its momentum in the Renaissance, when Boccaccio uses it in the *Decameron* to console people who are disappointed in love. *Who would want to be anywhere else* is a Renaissance thought. In the Middle Ages, everyone was headed to Paradise."

Freccero says that words in Dante's grammatology are links between the body and the soul. The Word in Christian thought is God. "In the Middle Ages," he says, "everyone was looking for the language gene." Freccero sees "language" as a synonym for "desire." Each time Dante talks about language, he is discussing how to live with desire and finally vanquish it and achieve satisfaction, Paradise on earth. "It is in the gap between need and desire that language is born." The infant acquires language through gesture, pointing at what it wants. Dante's journey is, in Freccero's sense, the journey to enlightened, disciplined, yet highly imaginative adulthood.

Freccero tells how Dante chose Virgil to guide him, rejecting another, his own celebrated Florentine teacher, Brunetto Latini, who had promised to teach Dante how to become eternal. When Dante meets him in *Inferno,* Brunetto recommends his book, *Li*

Livres dou tresor, or *Treasure* as it is referred to in English, an ency-clopedia. Dante is more shocked to find Brunetto in Hell than he was earlier to find Virgil there: *"Siete voi qui, ser Brunetto?"*—"Are you here, Ser Brunetto?" (*Inferno* 15.30) Brunetto has ended up in the circle of sodomites. "He doesn't belong there," says Freccero. "Like Socrates, Brunetto is accused of corrupting the young with false—backward—ideas about eternal happiness."

This is the first intimation that Dante is distancing himself from future history. He is rejecting the motifs of humanism which will dominate the Renaissance. Brunetto's book, of which he is so proud, suggests the false paradise of humanists, and Dante parts ways with the humanists. "A book like a child is not a great enough act in the desire for eternity. Dante is already noticing in *Purgatorio* that work is always being made and unmade; it is a gloss on the 'magnum volume' of God's book, which he will see in *Paradiso,*" Freccero says.

To become eternal through his art is not enough for Dante, who wants to reach perfection in God's eyes. The soul seeks not "eternal art" or the artifice of eternity, but its own eternity. The artist seeks eternity for his work. Dante seeks eternity for the soul made in the image and likeness of the Creator. The difference is between poetry and grace—or allegory: the many in the one.

Brunetto's sentence is to run endlessly—a race without a finish line. When he stops to talk to Dante, Brunetto "falls so far behind his own group that he seems to be leading the next." "Regression" in an aging teacher "can pass for leadership among the young," Freccero notes.

"Everybody wants immortality," says Freccero. "Most people accomplish this by making children, which is the immortality of the species, but not of the individual. A vulgar form of immortality, says Socrates. Indissolubly linked to reproduction in Dante's day is death. Socrates and Plato dismiss sexuality as an offering to death. A higher form is through philosophy and the individual spirit."

Brunetto disappeared in the book he authored. Dante will fail if he leaves behind merely a book. He wants to leave a vision of the human condition and its improvement. As T. S. Eliot, captivated by the image of Brunetto, wrote:

> By that refining fire
> Where you must learn to swim, and better nature.

"To call Brunetto Latini a homosexual," says Freccero, "is to distance ourselves from this old sunburnt man. Dante wants to walk reverently behind him, as he does Virgil. Brunetto was a great humanist of his time. Historians have besmirched Latini most by calling him 'worldly.' Yet Dante does the ghastly deed: he accuses Brunetto of this kind of vice. Dante talks about how grateful he is to Brunetto. This is a vicious irony: biting and stinging. Dante is condemning a certain kind of humanism: a purely secular kind. Brunetto, a humanist, ends up a loser who looks like a winner. The figure is that of a runner on a track and is outpaced. For a minute, he appears to be leading the pack, he is so far behind. A perfect figure for the aging guru whose arrested development makes him look like a leader."

No teacher is ever enough. Even Beatrice will disappear again, as Dante discovers.

PART IV

Paradiso (1316-21)

CHAPTER 10

What the Bread God Wished

IT SHOULD BE THAT THE MORE ONE TRIES TO KNOW GOD, the closer one gets to him. But this didn't seem true as Dante progressed through Italy. For a long time, he seemed to be going in the opposite direction. He found Bologna full of prostitutes and pimps (*Inferno* 18.57–63), Florence in league with Lucifer (*Paradiso* 9.127), Pistoia a den of beasts (*Inferno* 24.125–26), Genoa corrupt (*Inferno* 33.151–52). May the Arno be dammed at its mouth and drown all Pisa down to the last mouse (*Inferno* 33.79–84).

A story, popular in the thirteenth century, related that Adam was born outside of Eden and earned his entrance. It was called "opposite Eden." Man was made crude but was able to appreciate beauty and love and find grace. It implied that man was not meant to live in Eden, only to visit. Otherwise he would never know humility or grace.

All the roads appeared to lead away from home and repose. In Verona in 1315, Dante was offered asylum. Political offenders were permitted to return to Florence if they paid a greatly reduced portion of the original fine and thereby admitted the legitimacy of their sentence. After fifteen years of "unmerited exile," Dante wrote, how dare the city put him in the position of "some prisoner ransomed from just condemnation. . . . If I cannot enter Florence by an honorable path, I will not re-enter it at all."

In whatever corner of the world I find myself, can I not
look at the sun and stars? Can I not under any portion of
heaven meditate on the highest and sweetest truth
unless I make myself a man of shame, one dishonored
in the face of the people of Florence? I am confident I
shall never want for bread. (Epistle 10)

In October 1315, it is speculated, Dante left Verona for Lucca. In
1316, he traveled back to Verona. He rode by donkey through
Bagnacavallo—remarkable only because this town was in Black
Guelf territory, and Dante and his donkey were subjected to
insults and stones. The animal died and was buried there. Well
into the early 1900s, tourists who came to town were said to be
"searching for the bones of Dante's ass." In drawing up a list of
bastard sons who became princes, Dante said the town would do
well to castrate itself:

Ben fa Bangnacaval, che non rifiglia . . .

Bagnacavallo does well to have no more children . . .

Purgatorio. 14.115 (Merwin)

Dante was closer to Paradise than his experience in these Italian
towns suggests. "I'd have you disentangle yourself from this point
on, from fear and shame," Beatrice tells him as she greets him in
the Earthly Paradise, "so that you no longer speak like one who
dreams" (*Purgatorio* 33. 31–33). She means, stop making yourself
dull with false fantasy.

"... *e veggi vostra via da la divina*
distar contanto, quanto si discorda
da terra il ciel che più alto festina."

"as the earth is distant from
the highest and the swiftest of the heavens,
so distant is your way from the divine."

(33.88–90; trans. Mandelbaum)

She warns him,

"... *Veramente orami saranno nude*
le mie parole, quanto converrassi
quelle scovrire a la tua vista rude."

"... from now on the words I speak will be
naked; that is appropriate if they
would be laid bare before your still-crude sight."

(33.100–102; trans. Mandelbaum)

With her words, Dante feels "remade as new trees are renewed in bringing forth new boughs." He says at the end of *Purgatorio*, "I was pure and prepared to climb unto the stars" (33.143–45). He was ready to discover Paradise and would not leave Italy to do so.

In his last three years of exile, Dante's life is a poem. He finds Beatrice, she smiles upon him, and every strand of existence seems to marry, for a time, in the vault of heaven inside the solid Roman walls of Ravenna.

*

HE ARRIVES THERE by way of Verona. "In Verona," observed the art historian Arthur Symons, who traveled to Italy in the late 1800s, a copy of the *Commedia* in hand, "the gutters are of marble." The Renaissance turned dirt towns into showplaces. When Dante walked into Verona in 1315, it was a ruin, notes Symons, built for "cruel use." The Scaliger family had made it their headquarters as they planned and began executing the takeover of Vicenza, Feltre and, soon, Padua and Venice. The young lord of the clan, Francesco "Cangrande" della Scala, was the power of Verona and Dante's patron. The nickname Cangrande means "Big Dog." He is said never to be afraid of anything. His nephew would give their name to La Scala, the celebrated opera house in Milan. Cangrande died in an attempted coup of Venice in 1328, and all of Italy seemed to breathe a sigh of relief.

But when Cangrande first harbored the homeless poet, he was still in his twenties, having been born, it is believed, in 1291. He had already spent half his life extending his dominion. He was a patron of the arts, except that he treated his artists as pets. Dante found he had to share Cangrande's hospitality with a crowd of claimants to knowledge—historians, grammarians, astrologers and poets—who lived in little houses called "Fair Hope" or "The School of the Muses," each decorated with a painting of Paradise. Cangrade's older brother enjoyed deflating the artists' pretensions. Pointing to a jester, he told Dante, "I am astonished that one of the fools has gained the favor of everyone, while you who are said to be wise cannot do the same." Dante replied: "You should not be astonished, for friendship attracts similar manners and similar intelligence." Osip Mandelstam wrote, "If the halls of the

Hermitage were suddenly to go mad, if the paintings of all the schools and great masters were suddenly to break loose from their nails and merge with one another, intermingle and fill the air of the rooms with a roar and an agitated frenzy of color, we would then have something resembling Dante's *Commedia*." Closer still, we would have a spectacle of the boisterous distractions of the Cangrande court.

Not that Dante wasn't grateful. He dedicated *Paradiso* to Cangrande:

> I have carefully looked over the little things that I could give you, and separated and examined them each by each, seeking the most worthy and pleasing for you. Nor did I find anything more suitable for your preeminence than the sublime canticle of the Comedy which is called Paradise; which I inscribe, offer and commend to you. (*Epistle to Cangrande* 10)

Dante left Verona, however, as soon as the opportunity arose, and that opportunity was an invitation in 1318 from the son of Guido Novello da Polenta, lord of Ravenna, to settle in this city on the Adriatic coast. There was the offer of a house of his own and work befitting his prestige as the celebrated author of *Inferno*. Dante became the first professor to teach poetry in the vulgar. What is astonishing is that Novello, "the Eagle of Polenta" (*L'Aquila da Polenta*), bore no grudge against Dante for putting his aunt, Francesca da Rimini, in Hell (*Inferno 5*), spinning with her adulterous lover Paolo for all the ages. It is perhaps a testimony to Dante's fame. Or perhaps Guido didn't care, because Dante's presence was an investment in Ravenna.

Dante arrived stooped, grave and dignified. His long nose and his long face weighed down by a heavy jaw, he was bearded and sunburned. Perhaps Ravenna looked somber to Dante. The Roman Empire was born there and died there. Strange—it had the whole world to die in and chose that obscure place in the marshes.

*

IF THIS WERE a Borges story, full of the twists where author and character change places, we would pause and suggest that God, the Divine Poet, had created a character named Dante, by which He tries to explain Himself. We might ask why Dante's God is made in the image of Narcissus? God is a self-conscious artist. He knows and expresses himself as Dante. If God embraces everyone, he also embraces Himself in love—in the Trinity, as Aquinas tells us. And in the *Comedy*.

By the end of *Paradiso*, Dante's goal is to experience unmediated, absolute reality. No filters; no poetical reality. Not a few pretty images of Heaven, but rather the full pleasure of life neither minimized nor made ironical in any safe way. This sight is only allowed the godlike. We see Dante's likeness to God: the poet creates "Dante" as God creates the cosmos. Dante wants us to know that at the very least God has given his sacred approval to the *Comedy*.

Carl Jung said that God used Job to solve a crisis in self-identity. By inflicting suffering on one of His creatures, He was proving His case for justice. In creating Dante, God seems to experiment with love as the vehicle for the intellect: two human forces, genius and sweetness, that had not yet been paired in history.

There are no self-portraits in the Middle Ages. One hundred years after Dante died, Leon Battista Alberti in his treatise on painting defined self-regard, or the Narcissus myth, positively. He was the first to do so: "What else does painting do but reflect the surface of art and love?"

*

RAVENNA IS A secret Paradise. Even today it is one of the least visited cities in northern Italy. Florence was singular as the birthplace of an intellectual and artistic era unsurpassed in the history of the West. But Ravenna was granted a more illustrious heritage: the marriage and parting of eastern Christianity and the West. It is said that in Ravenna men had a Roman body, a Greek mind and an oriental, mystical soul: all three traditions meet in what Augustus called "the city in the sea."

"Three times Western civilization has been shaped in the city of Ravenna," wrote the art historian Otto von Simson. "In 49 B.C., Caesar gathered his followers at its port before crossing the Rubicon. He thus tied the city to the fortunes of the Roman empire." In 1321, Dante would die in Ravenna, having completed the *Comedy* inside its walls. "The eyes which had been the last to behold the vision of the imperium in its glory closed where Caesar had prepared its foundation," wrote Simson. Between Caesar and Dante, in the fifth century, the Emperor Honorius moved his residence from Rome to Ravenna—then a fortress city protected from attack by the water and devious lagoons. Honorius and his half-sister Galla Placidia made love and quarreled within its walls. Similarly, enemies from the different camps of God, from East and West, appeared to embrace each other in Ravenna.

It was an untenable alliance. The embrace and subsequent clash occurred over the Greek-Byzantine conception of God and western thought. Greek Arianism had sought to strip Christ of his divinity. Had this movement won out, Greek philosophy would have conquered western theology. The rational Greek philosophy would have destroyed the mystical experience of redemption. Essentially the clash was over the reality of Paradise. "We remember Jesus over the horde of would-be messiahs preaching at street corners throughout the Roman republic," says the scholar Stephen Shoemaker, "because His story unlike the others included a resurrection—a return from death—hell, and a new life in the light."

It was the force of this mystery, the incomprehensibility of it, that won Christ the world. Christ had absorbed the ancient Orient into his teachings as well as all the dark conception of prehistoric times. He was the bread god, dead and reborn with the seasons. All the images of a Messiah survived in the one who told his followers they could eat His body and experience transcendence. He is the agrarian lord of seed born in Beth-Lehem, which means "House of Bread," and He is the god of wine. The Greeks honored him as Bacchus, bound to the wood. He is the Second Coming of the Greek Adonis who was killed by the boar. He spilled his blood among the roses and was lamented by women. This continuous return from the dead in life and legend, ending up with eternal life in Paradise, enabled Christ to become the historical Messiah.

No city embodied the spirit of the two worlds, West and East, as dramatically as Ravenna. The Empress Placidia built the greatest Byzantine churches, Santa Croce and San Giovanni Evangelista—they were offerings in thanks for being saved when her boat barely made it ashore from a storm on the Adriatic Sea. Venice and Rome were crowded with churches dedicated to the Virgin Mary or Jesus. Ravenna churches celebrated martyrs like Apollinaris, the archbishop of Ravenna in 468, who spent his life giving away his silver, hoping his mystical visions would sway politics, and finally, when his suffering became great, asked to be hung in a martyr's death. In the churches, the mosaics wrested a vision of transcendence from the raw material of life. The figures walk on air yet seem human, and they seem conscious of being observed. In churches in the other cities of Dante's travels, the mosaics portray the dogma of religion: Christ, Mary, the disciples. But in Ravenna, mortal figures with ravenously big eyes and faces, childlike and mature at the same time, make a worshiper feel like a potential dweller in Paradise. The figures under the "tent of heaven" are human. Ravenna is the home of the drama of human transformation.

Here, aligned with the house of Polenta, Dante could live as though Paradise loomed.

*

PARADISO IS THE canticle of desire fulfilled. Dante described how he saw perfection, experienced bliss and satisfied his wants. As John Freccero concludes: "The irony of the human condition is that desire is insatiable and purely natural. *But the satisfaction of it is supernatural.*"

What happens to Dante in Paradise? He knows, experiences, and understands love. And once he does, he falls back down to earth, accepts his human limits—and in a bold effort, writes the *Comedy,* the very book we are reading. "There is no humor in this

man, but love was there till misfortune turned it into theology,"
wrote Thomas Carlyle.

The question that has brought Dante on this quest is laid bare:
"Do you love me?" Or to put it perhaps more modernly: "Am I
worthy of being loved?" "What can I do to be worthy of being
loved?" The answer in Paradise is to open yourself to love and
return it. Dante considers this life's most difficult work. The first
neologism in *Paradiso* is *transumanar:* to go beyond, in this case to
transcend the human limits to that which cannot be put in human
words (*Paradiso* 1.70–71).

The ambition for everything other than love is silenced in Paradise. There is no desire. Each soul is perfectly happy according to
his potential to know happiness. There is no envy, no striving.
What makes these souls different from the damned in Hell is not
that they have not sinned but that they have found repentance,
love and grace. The spirit, Folquet of Marseille, appears as "joy"
(9.70–78). He doesn't merely greet Dante at a distance, as the souls
in Hell and Purgatory have done. Folquet can enter into Dante as
joy enters a person (9.81). He tells Dante that since the soul in Paradise is one with God, it shares His omniscience. Folquet therefore knows exactly what is on Dante's mind:

> *Qui si rímina ne l'arte ch' addorna*
> *cotanto affetto, e discernesi 'l bene*
> *per che 'l mondo di sù quel di giù torna.*

> Here all our thoughts are fixed upon the love
> That beautifies creation, and here we learn
> how world below is moved by world above.

> (*Paradiso* 9.106–8; trans. Ciardi)

And so beginning at the moon, Dante ascends through the nine heavens beyond space and time. As Hell was composed of hierarchical levels of evil or misinterpretation, and Purgatory was built of terraces where art increasingly turned its editing techniques on the maker, not the thing made, so Paradise consists of spheres leading to the center of the cosmos: God.

In one of these heavens, Dante hears Thomas Aquinas but cannot see him, the light is too strong. Grace produces love, Thomas tells him, and love has grown within Dante so much that he can now mount through the spheres. Thomas introduces the other lights: Solomon, author of the ecstatic Song of Songs; Dionysius, the symbol of wisdom rooted in desire; and the Franciscan Saint Bonaventure, another philosopher of love.

Dante sees eternity: the point at which all time is present at once (17.17–18). Beatrice is in the lead. Dante accepts the most adult love of his life. But Beatrice warns him "paradise is not only in my eyes" (18.21). The passion of earthly love is a valuable token of divine love, but a token merely.

Halfway through Paradise (17.58), Dante encounters his spiritual master, Cacciaguida—his name means "guide of the hunt"— who prophesies that his great-great-great-grandson, Dante, will know exile; he will eat the salty bread of others, and discover how hard a path it is to climb down and up another's stairs. Dante learns about his ancestry, the history of the cities of Italy, by talking to this distant ancestor. The scope of this lesson is self-knowledge; and it endows Dante with a sense of prophecy. He has a vision that he will die young. Cacciaguida is too deep for Dante. His long absorption into the divine intellect has made natural to him modes of thought beyond mortal understanding. Yet he makes himself understood. He reminds Dante that he is living a comedy, not a tragedy: Go down and tell them the truth, he says, and let them scratch where it itches. Dante's powers of feeling outrun his powers of utterance. He promises Cacciaguida he will hold nothing back. He becomes a poet who is a warrior. He can thank Cacciaguida only with his heart.

Dante soars up through the fourth heaven, Mercury. Then, the fifth heaven, Mars. The sixth, Jupiter. He sees souls form words in the sky (18.70–72): David, Hezekiah, Trajan—just leaders who become one creature, an eagle. The seventh heaven is Saturn's. Dante ascends the stairway to delight. Beatrice does not smile here lest the radiance turn Dante to dust. This is the heaven of contemplative monastics such as Peter Damian, who "enwombs himself" in love: *"m'inventro"* (21.84).

The higher Dante goes, the more homely the images (21.115). By the time he reaches the eighth heaven, a blink of Beatrice's eye (22.101) transports Dante to the sphere of the fixed stars. He looks back down to earth—"so pitiful of semblance that it moved my smiles." His sight improves as he ascends.

At each heaven, he feels his limits: slowly he cracks out of his boundaries like a butterfly out of a cocoon. He strains against his failure and the failure of all languages to imagine God (23.61–63). All we can know about God is that we can know nothing about Him. Dante sees that the soul strains upward as babies stretch their arms to their mothers (23.121). Encountering St. Peter, he remarks that Peter no longer needs faith because he sees what he used only to believe (24.63–64): "Faith is the substance of the things we hope for and is evidence of things not seen." Peter tells Dante that Pope Boniface will never receive mercy. History will always be resolved in justice. The movements of the mind and the planets achieve a kind of music and harmony.

By the ninth heaven, Dante, blinded by the light, sees how God is the true author of the cosmos. God is more essentially love than faith or hope. With this revelation, Dante's sight is restored. He can see Beatrice again. She will now "imparadise" his mind— "*quella che 'mparadisa la mia mente*" (28.3). And then he reaches the Primum Mobile: the rim of the wheel on which Heaven spins. Language must leap to describe Dante's experiences in the Primum Mobile, which has no space, time or physical being. *Paradiso* scholar Jeffrey Burton Russell wrote: "If a spoon or a plant 'exist,' then the empyrean does not. . . . and if *it* 'exists,' *they* do not."

The moral center of Heaven is not judgment but love. It is more than beauty; it is light, the substance of love that warms and discloses and penetrates. Dante sees the shape of the cosmos. It is laid out like a stadium for all the beautiful souls, a rose (30.117). The tiers of seats look like the petals of a rose. All the fires he has seen and felt resolve themselves at this height of perception into a sweet red rose, the symbol of love.

At last, he has arrived at the task he has traveled all this way to accomplish—the chance to tell Beatrice what he could not say on earth:

> *Tu m'hai di servo tratto a libertate*
> *per tutte quelle vie, per tutt'i modi*
> *che di ciò fare avei la potestate.*

> You have led me from my bondage and set me free
>   by all those roads, by all those loving means
>   that lay within your power and charity.

di tante cose quant' i' ho vedute,
  dal tuo podere e da la tua bontate
  riconosco la grazia e la virtute.

through your power and your excellence alone
  have I recognized the goodness and the grace
  inherent in the things I have been shown.

> (*Paradiso* 31.85–87, 31.82–84;
>
> trans. Ciardi)

It is perfectly simple. There is no pronouncement of love, only goodness and grace. The nearer Dante approaches in God's lofty presence, the more simple the poet becomes.

And then Dante addresses God—who is the light in a singular star (31.28)—and begs to see more. He turns to Beatrice for help, but to his surprise he finds in her place an old man, Bernard of Clairvaux, crusader, mystic, reformer—Dante's third and final guide. Beatrice had tried to show Dante Heaven. Bernard knows it cannot be shown. "Where is she?" Dante cries, *"Ov'è ella?"* (31.64) He sees that Beatrice is where she has always been, in the third rank of Heaven, below Mary, John, Peter, Adam and Moses. Dante cannot speak to her anymore. But she speaks to him. Beatrice invites Dante to look directly at God.

What permits Dante to have that vision? He has followed the traces of grace in the universe, and all these have led him to come face-to-face with God. The suggestion is that anyone could follow the same track and see the meaning of the universe.

Dante's sight and understanding expand and he enters deeper into the light that is Truth (33.52–54). Bernard guides him in how to complete the journey into the self, the pure realm of the mind, where sensual experience becomes more delicate, more true and more fulfilling, where each event is consummation. He is beyond Aquinas now, beyond the knowledge that the senses foster. For most of us, there is no such thing as an immaterial thought. Dante appears to achieve it.

And here is what he finally sees: all the scattered diversity of the universe as fallen leaves, gathered and bound in one volume, a book in which every letter has meaning, all words the Word that worshipers call God, Logos (33.85–87 and 33.130–31). God moves him (33.143–45). *"Oh ineffabile allegrezza!"*—"O joy beyond words."

It is said that Dante put his enemies in Hell and his friends in Paradise. In fact, *Paradiso* unites three quests: for love, for the language with which to express love and for God, the exemplar of love. They join in the roads to Paradise, where we learn that love gives us the power of gods.

Beatrice is for Dante only the second guide in this quest, not its object. The canticle may look like the story of sweethearts beyond the grave. But it isn't. Beatrice leaves him in Paradise. Fittingly, perhaps, for there is no evidence that she loved him nearly as much as he loved her. There is no evidence in fact that she noticed Dante during life. If we are looking for a point, Freccero suggests it may be that "love, thanks to grace, outdistances our ability to understand."

The erotic climax carries a bigger wallop than two old lovers meeting. Throughout *Paradiso,* the images illustrate the complex relationship of soul and church, male and female, seeker and the artist of living. The height of the erotic is reached in Canto 10 in this supposedly ethereal poem. This canto is a hymn to the Trinity, and to love, in the form of a meditation on the sun. It depicts the embrace of two (human) lovers and Dante's journey from prepubescent cravings to transcendence. But images like this run throughout. "A pearl on a milk-white brow" is the image of Dante as he loses himself in the erotic imagination: a total possession as white disappears in white. The memory is of a jewel young Tuscan women wore on their foreheads. In this image, Dante stops learning and becomes part of the process of grace.

One can imagine oneself in this spiritual eros of Paradise when, approaching a glass building, one sees oneself. That is the impression of *Paradiso*. There is a sense in which Paradise is all surface. The glance that is the reflected glance—*looking at;* and the refracted glance—*looking back* to what lies beyond the glass. Souls appear and disappear as if moving through water. They merge into one another, losing their individual identity to fill the glass itself.

Near to its final vision, the body, Dante writes, swells in love: *"spirito d'amor turge"*—the sanctification of human sexuality. Love, he sees, is God and man as one.

*

LOVE IS ALSO language at its absolute: Dante's *"amorosa lima,"* the "loving file," he says, had "polished his speech." Dante has found a language that is as enveloping as silence, language free of language's limits to convey pure light without the shadow of words. Or has he? "Language is desire," Freccero points out. "The infant points to what he wants or needs. Dante is aiming at bliss, the fulfillment of all needs."

As the poet moves upward, his words fall behind . . . until in Canto 33, line 55, *il parlar nostro,* human discourse, they fail utterly.

Da quinci innanzi il mio veder fu maggio
  che 'l parlar mostra, ch'a tal vista cede,
  e cede la memoria a tanto oltraggio.

What then I saw is more than tongue can say.
  Our human speech is dark before the vision.
  The ravished memory swoons and falls away.

                              (trans. Ciardi)

This effort to transcend language is what makes *Paradiso*
Dante's most modern work. Dante describes his inability to write
as *Paradiso* begins:

La gloria di colui che tutto move
  per l'universo penetra, e risplende
  in una parte più e meno altrove.

Nel ciel che più de la sua luce prende
  fu'io, e vidi cose che ridire
  né sa né può chi di là sù discende . . .

The glory of Him who moves all things rays forth
  through all the universe, and is reflected
  from each thing in proportion to its worth . . .

I have been in that Heaven of His most light
  and what I saw, those who descend from there
  lack both the knowledge and the power to write.

                              (1.1–6; trans. Ciardi)

But he tries still and reaches the point when he declares his vocation as that of a scribe: the *Comedy* has been written in his heart. Dante is not a *postilla*, or footnote. He is at least a palimpsest. The text is God.

★

DANTE RELIES ON sight, the king of the senses. He surrenders to it. The human body lives like other organisms by touch. "On the other side," Dante tells us, "all is seeing and seeing is all. One accepts one's blindness and limited understanding in Dante's *Paradiso*, as never before," says Freccero.

On Straw Street in Paris, Dante had learned that astronomy was "the surest of sciences." Physics cannot hope for reliability; its world is always in flux. Theology deals with things beyond sight and understanding. Astronomy helps to sharpen the eyes of the mind and intellect to consider those things whose movements most resemble the divine in their moderation, balance and lack of excess. Dante wrote more than one hundred passages on astronomy in the *Commedia*. He called the stars' influence "the government of the world," believing that heavenly bodies influence the earth: tides and light tug at oceans, nourish crops and direct people's actions. The essence of the problem of cosmology is the problem of God's place in the universe, says Freccero. There is no center: the more you try to approach the (dead, still) center, the more you fail. You never reach a point without motion. Dante pushes his majestic nose further into the universe than anyone of his time.

★

DANTE WAS JOINED in his last refuge of Ravenna by his son Pietro, a successful lawyer in Verona. His elder son, Jacopo, banished in the same decree of 1302 and denied the same pardon offered in 1315, had also moved to Ravenna. His daughter, Beatrice, whom he had last seen when she was a baby, came to stay with him and take care of him.

Dante's efforts were taken up with *Paradiso* until Ravennese sailors attacked a Venetian ship in 1321. Control the mouth of the Ravenna canal and one controlled the vast wealth in shipping. Ravenna became the leader in transportation of salt, more precious than gold because it kept food edible. Cities revolted when salt was unavailable. Venetians would tolerate no threat to their passage in these waters. They soon formed an alliance and declared war upon Ravenna and its lord, Guido Novello da Polenta. The neighboring republics of Cesena, Imola and Faenza were put on notice: anyone in alliance with Guido was Venice's enemy. Forlì supplied 200 cavalry sworn to Ravenna's defeat. Ravenna was threatened on all sides. In late August, Guido sent Dante to Venice.

The Venice that Dante saw we may see through the eyes of Ezra Pound. He saw in Venice an inverted light. Venetian light, said Pound, was "not of the sun," and its stone forests were not of the order of nature. It is the most completely ambiguous of sacred places, the most wholly an assertion of sheer will.

Dante's mission failed. A letter, of uncertain authenticity, was written to Guido, perhaps by Dante, reporting on the events. Having begun his discussions in Latin, Dante says he was told to stop because the language was foreign to the Venetians. He tried his Florentine mother tongue and was told the Venetians could not understand. He begged Guido never to send him on a similar mission. A contemporary noted that the Venetians refused to listen to Dante, fearing that the power of his eloquence would unravel the resolve of the alliance.

Perhaps the Venetians were not impressed that Guido had sent a poet as his surrogate and paid Dante little heed. The state archives for the year 1321 have been lost, but it is believed that Dante discussed navigation rights along the Po, the river that begins in the Italian Alps and flows across the green pastures of Emilia-Romagna into Ravenna and finally into Venice. The primacy of land and sea was a subject Dante had recently studied. When the time came to return to Ravenna with his delegation, Venice refused to grant him a safe conduct by the most convenient route. He made his way back through malarial swampland and caught a fever.

On his way home, Dante was greeted by the Benedictine fathers at Fonte Avellana on Monte Catria. The delegation passed through the lagoons of Comacchio, crossed the Lamone, and entered the northern reaches of the Pineta, a pine forest. Once home, Dante lived for three days, dying on September 14, 1321. By his wish, he was buried in the habit of a Franciscan friar.

A second delegation was sent in October, one month after Dante's death. That envoy suggested that Venice draw up the articles of the peace treaty—essentially a capitulation.

*

BOCCACCIO WROTE: "It was a habit with Dante, as soon as he had finished six or eight cantos [of the *Commedia*], before anyone else had seen them, to send them to Can Grande della Scala, whom he esteemed more than any other living man, and as soon as he had seen them, Dante would then make a copy for anyone else who wished for it. In this way, having sent him all but the last thirteen cantos—these being done but not yet sent—Dante died. His sons and other disciples searched for them for months . . . lamenting that God had not lent him a little longer to the world so as to enable him to complete his work." Jacopo then had a dream in which his father appeared. He asked his father if he were still alive, and Dante said "he was alive with a true life—not this of ours." He asked about the missing cantos and was told they were in a wall niche behind the stove in his bedroom. Upon awakening, Jacopo found the missing cantos precisely where his father's shade had said they were. Even today, some think Jacopo concocted this story.

*

JOHN FRECCERO NOTES that "in Italy, Dante is the father of the country, as George Washington is here. The poet is in this image a new warrior. In Italy, every town has in its center a statue of Dante."

After his death, Florence wanted Dante back. "Ah! The shame of having to record that a mother was envious of her own child," Boccaccio vituperated to the city fathers. "He [Dante] cannot do to Florence dead what living he would never have done. . . . Hardly can I believe that, if dead bodies are capable of feeling, that of Dante would wish to leave the place where it lies now to return to you." Ravenna, Boccaccio said, "bathed in the blood of martyrs, is a more hospitable home."

Guido staged a contest for a design of a fitting burial place for Dante. Not long after his bones were assumed to be safely in the ground, the Florentines moved in and tried to dig up the corpse of Dante Alighieri. On December 22, 1396, Florence made a formal demand for his remains. Ravenna refused. Another demand came on February 1, 1492, and a third refusal came in 1529, when Michelangelo offered to build a tomb for "the divine poet." Then an official party was dispatched. It was the bad luck of the magistrate of Ravenna that he had that month refused to pay the enormous salaries of the Papal Swiss Guard, and the pope, Leo X, had held them in Cesena, leaving Ravenna undefended. The Florentine envoys arrived in the dead of night and raised the stone lid of Dante's tomb. To their astonishment, they found it empty, except for a few bone chips and withered laurel leaves. Their report concluded:

> It being believed that in his lifetime [Dante] made the journey through Inferno, Purgatorio and Paradiso, so in death it must now be assumed that in body as well as in spirit in either one or other of the realms he has been received and welcomed.

So the matter was left until, in 1890, documentation was found that a Franciscan had, centuries earlier, broken into the sarcophagus and removed the bones for safekeeping elsewhere in Ravenna. The records reveal where the monk hid Dante's remains. Once recovered, they were put on display in Ravenna for three days, from June 24 to 26, 1890. People came from everywhere to say they had seen the great Dante Alighieri. On June 27, all that could be buried of Dante was entombed in a great white vault surrounded by a tiny garden in Ravenna.

*

DANTE'S LAST VISION in *Paradiso* was of love, as Canto 33, the one hundredth of the *Comedy*, says:

l'amor che move il sole e l'altre stelle.

the Love that moves the Sun and the other stars.

(146; Ciardi trans.)

Each canticle of the *Commedia* ends with Dante's view of the stars. In *Inferno*, he and Virgil take a hidden road back to the faint glimmerings of the stars. In *Purgatorio*, he is "pure and ready to ascend to the stars." Freccero says of the final vision of *Paradiso* that *amor* is the last word of the poem: love is the ending of the journey. While Dante is beginning this line, he is already looking up at the stars, falling toward earth. When he utters this line, he is back to where he began: alone in the dark wood, line 1, Canto 1, *Inferno*. It is the brilliance of Dante's trek that he returns from this experience to human limits and writes.

Why does Dante end here? He becomes Dante the pilgrim and Dante the poet as well as the philosopher and theologian—and he is now ready to write this poem. As the critic William Cook says, the best way to read the *Comedy* is first as a seeker, next as a poet and creator.

★

DANTE'S WHOLE JOURNEY in Paradise has been the quest to go beyond language, to see what cannot be written. He makes his peace with the limitations of the flesh. Until the last stages of

Dante's journey, his was a faith seeking understanding. His last vision was the fulfillment of the soul's desires and an integration with the rest of creation. The intellect, in knowing God, knows all that it can possibly know. The will is made perfect in willing itself to love. Dante has finally become what Guido Cavalcanti said he was, those many years ago, when they were young men in Florence asserting the link between sweetness and greatness: *"Dante, un sospiro messagger del core"*—"Dante, you are a sigh, like a messenger of the heart."

Love pulled too at the mind of Aquinas in his last days. Critics say he was too intellectual about everything, that he saw satisfaction as the love of truth rather than as the truth of love. Thomas Aquinas had had his last quarrel with the Parisian rationalist, Siger of Brabant, in 1274. Siger argued for the idea of a mortal body and soul and threatened to end all idea of religion, Thomas believed. After that fight, something happened to Thomas. He said, "I can write no more. I have seen things which make all my writings like straw." It was his own struggle with language and silence—and silence won. Aquinas was near fifty. On a last mission for the pope, he came down with a sudden sickness. Dying, he asked to have the Song of Solomon read to him, which shocked his brother monks. As G. K. Chesterton imagined the scene, Aquinas's brothers must have felt at that moment that "the inside of the monastery was larger than the outside." Ideas were at play inside this great mind that Thomas had never entertained before. The confessor who heard his last words said that his confession "had been that of a child of five."

★

WAVERLY ROOT IN *The Food of Italy* asks, "Does a well-fed race produce more geniuses than others?" Perhaps he was thinking of all the explorers, artists, musicians and strategists raised on Italian plenty. Even America has an Italian name. We ourselves are nouveau Romans. So, did Dante ever eat well? More than a bit of beef and a sip of wine? Did all the sweetness he sought come from the endless rhymes in his mouth? Dante presumably tasted Paradise in Ravenna as nowhere else. Guido was a generous host, and Ravenna is an ocean of feast: hogfish, eel, lemon sole, grey mullet, red mullet, dogfish, squill, *calamari* and *mazzole*. The Pinetà, the pine forest, yielded pine nuts for desserts; the shells added fragrance to fires.

Dante had been a beggar for most of his life in exile. But the matters of gods and stomachs assume new importance at the end of *Paradiso,* written at the close of the High Middle Ages. The age's towering achievements would also descend back to a dark wood, as if Dante's vision bore literal truth. From the sign of Gemini, his birth star, up in Paradise, Dante looked down through the seven heavens to see the far-distant outline of the world:

l'aiuola che ci fa tanto feroci

the little threshing floor that makes us so fierce . . .

(22.151; trans. Frecerro)

The bread god was now writing a new script. Paradise—named for dough—*par-dheigh*—a shaped and risen world of manna—was drifting far away. Famine was approaching Europe. Hunger had been a constant in the lives of the medievals. It was believed that "the devil dwelt in the mill." All the people of the Middle Ages, Dante included, had a hatred for the miller's trade. Millers were known to shortchange merchants in weight of the grain. At the lowest circle of the Inferno (Canto 34), Dante sees a windmill turning in the dark. It had "no feathers" and looked like a bat, but in fact it is the devil. Bakers were distrusted too.

In the remaining years of the 1320s, starvation contributed to the Plague's devastation. The achievements of man paled with the scarcity of bread. The first publication of Dante's *Vision,* as the *Comedy* was originally called, would not appear until 1472, as life was slowly returning from the destruction of the Plague and the Renaissance was about to be born.

Dantean Journey

The creator of the Lord Peter Whimsey novels, Dorothy Sayers, translated the *Comedy,* and five years before she died began a novel called *Dante's Daughter.* The story is based on fact as Boccaccio tells it. But Sayers takes it in a whole different direction, one that makes a Dantean-size leap, and therefore just might be true.

In 1371, Boccaccio was appointed by Florence the first official "exponent" of the *Commedia.* He attests that Dante was joined by his seventeen-year-old daughter in Ravenna. Sayers adds a twist: Daughter Beatrice has a vision in which she sees that her namesake never loved her father. She tells Dante this, and he struggles to understand whether the *Comedy* is based upon a lie. If Beatrice did not love him, then his work and search for redemption are false. One can see why Sayers never finished the novel. Fragments suggest a story fraught with incestuous undertones. Beatrice arrives at her father's door like a love-struck vision. Unlike the Beatrice of Dante's imagination, this daughter is his true love.

But it is possible that Sayers was exploring the most perplexing element of Dante's search for his genius. Is love *love* if it is not reciprocated? Or is the height of Paradise to love without reciprocation? Dante's Beatrice smiles at him at the end of *Paradiso* and then disappears. Is love supposed to disappear just when one finds it? Plato has an answer to this: *wine*. Do we not love wine and quail and art too, and never ask for these to love us in return? The love that needs no demonstration, no thanks, no reciprocity: this is the highest love and the one that is closest to God.

Following Sayers, one may ask: What if Dante's daughter is the real and only Beatrice? We know from Shakespeare the image of the maiden phoenix. In *King Lear,* one daughter redeems the father. In Shakespeare's life as in Dante's, he is reunited with his daughters. When Shakespeare goes back to Stratford and rejoins his two daughters, he quickly abandons military plays and the theme of honor. Shakespeare no longer follows the structure of power, the struggle of soldier and king. He writes instead *The Tempest, A Midsummer Night's Dream, King Lear, Cymbeline,* and *Pericles*—his "daughter" plays.

After Dante's death, his daughter entered the Convent of San Stefano degli Ulivi. Boccaccio found her there in 1353 when he brought her Dante's pension of ten gold florins, Florence's reparations for the injustice the poet had suffered. There is no further word of this Beatrice, nor what she did with this small fortune.

From a plaque on an old red wall, overlooking the public gardens:

> Beatrice, daughter of Dante Aligheri, in this convent of Santo Stefano degli Olivi, devoted herself to God, wroth with the world's wickedness, having seen her father through the evil dissension of citizens, condemned to perpetual exile, and to become a beggar for the bread of strangers.

Envoi: The Happy Ending

"IN THE END IS MY BEGINNING," wrote T. S. Eliot, "and in the beginning is my end." He is following Dante's return to earth in the last lines of the *Comedy* and the renewal of the journey. Happiness is the chance—or the choice—to start life over, to return to Hell stronger, to pass through Purgatory lighter, to reach Paradise closer to perfection. Dante at the end has promised a greater happiness, and this is it.

Notes

BIBLIOGRAPHIC NOTE: This book draws on the work of dozens of Dante scholars, chiefly John Freccero, Robert Hollander, Giuseppe Mazzotta, and Erich Auerbach, and on medieval histories, principally by Jacques Le Goff. Citations of their work and others' appear below, keyed to a fact or quotation in the preceding pages.

Passages from the *Comedy* are from translations by John Ciardi, Allen Mandelbaum, Robert Pinsky, W. S. Merwin and Philip Wicksteed. I quote them variously to give the reader the benefit of some of the best of Dante's poetry in English.

Chapter One

6 *The decree condemns the faction:* Allen Mandelbaum, "Dante in His Age," in Allen Mandelbaum, Anthony Oldcorn and Charles Ross, eds., *Lectura Dantis: Inferno* (Berkeley: University of California Press, 1998), p. 5.

6 *The idea of a united Italy is unimagined:* John Larner, *Italy in the Age of Dante and Petrarch 1216–1380* (London: Longman, 1980), p. 1.

8 Scholars do not agree on the origin of Guelfs and Ghibellines. G. Vilaini, *Cronica* 6.38, states that these were the names of castles in Germany, and the fighting began among them.

9 Habits of the Guelfs and Ghibellines, in John Addington Symons, *The Renaissance in Italy,* vol. 1 (New York: Henry Holt, 1908), p. 73–74.

9 Ghibelline brains and Frederick II history, in Ernest Kantorowicz, *Frederick the Second: 1194–1250,* trans. E. O. Lorimer (New York: Ungar, 1957), p. 67.

10 Boccaccio quotation, in Kantorowicz, p. 67.

10 Destruction of Florence, in Will Durant, *The Age of Faith: A History of Medieval Civilization—Christian, Islamic, and Judaic—from Constantine to Dante,* A.D. 325–1300 (New York: Simon & Schuster), p. 731.

11 Medieval cities, in Marc L. B. Bloch, *Feudal Society,* trans. L. A. Manyon (Chicago: University of Chicago Press, 1964), pp. 72–75.

12 The difficulties of exile in 1302, in Larner, p. 3.

12 *no common language:* Scholars agree on the point, though some regard this as overstating the case, citing *Convivio* I.3, 4.

12 Ethico, in Kantorowicz, p. 67.

12 Children's Crusade, in Kantorowicz, p. 59.

13 Dante's itinerary, in Thomas Caldecot Chubb, *Dante and His World* (Boston: Little, Brown, 1966), pp. 455–521.

14 Fish story, in Chubb, p. 498.

14 Medieval suppers, in Waverly Root, *The Food of Italy* (New York: Vintage, 1992), p. 34ff.

14 Dante's thievery, in Paget Jackson Toynbee, *Dante Alighieri* (London: Methuen, 1924).

15 Gods and solitude, in Umberto Eco, *Foucault's Pendulum,* trans. William Weaver (New York: Ballantine Books, 1990), p. 61.

16 Dante and reason, in Allen Chavkin, ed., *Conversations with John Gardner* (Jackson: University Press of Mississippi, 1990), p. 85.

19 Medieval economy, in Larner, p. 260ff.

19 *"we think medievally":* Dantista Simone Marchesi of Princeton warns against the lure of believing everything modern can be explained by medieval thought. Romanticism appropriated medieval imagery and altered it, he says: " 'I' is, today, and thanks to the Romantics, not equal to 'us.' 'I' was, for Dante—thanks to Christian Humanism—equal to 'us.' If this was not the case, how do you explain the force of the adjective 'our' in the first line of the *Comedy?"*

19 *"it is not surprising":* Umberto Eco, *Travels in Hyperreality: Essays,* trans. William Weaver (San Diego: Harcourt Brace, 1986), p. 65.

22 Dante and Scrooge, from John Freccero, class notes.

Chapter Two

24 *make words bleed:* Matthew Pearl, *The Dante Club* (New York: Random House, 2003), p. ix.

27 George Eliot story in Gordon S. Haight, *George Eliot: A Biography* (London: Penguin Books, 1992), p. 544; and Prof. Betty Sue Flowers, personal communication.

28 Gabriele Rossetti story in Peter Partner, *The Murdered Magicians: The Templars and Their Myth* (Oxford: Oxford University Press, 1982), p. 10.

28 Manuscript distribution, in Robert Hollander, *Dante: A Life in Works* (New Haven: Yale University Press, 2001), p. 92.

29 Freya Stark's travel items in, Jane Fletcher Geniesse, *Passionate Nomad: The Life of Freya Stark* (New York: Random House, 1999), p. 3.

30 *One disappeared into words:* Ivan Illich, *In the Vineyard of the Text: A Commentary to Hugh's* Didascalicon (Chicago: University of Chicago Press, 1993), p. 119.

30 Dante's rhythm, in Teodolinda Barolini, *The Undivine Comedy: Detheologizing Dante* (Princeton: Princeton University Press, 1992), pp. 24–25.

33 Social change, in Caroline Walker Bynum, *Jesus as Mother: Studies in the Spirituality of the High Middle Ages* (Berkeley: University of California Press, 1982), pp. 89–102.

33 Giovanni Boccaccio, *Life of Dante,* trans. James Robinson Smith (New York: Holt, 1901), pp. 42–43.

34 Joseph Campbell, *The Power of Myth* (New York: Doubleday, 1992).

34 *"living medicine":* "Conversations About Dante," in Jane Gary Harris, *Mandelstam: Critical Prose and Letters* (Ann Arbor: Ardis, 1990), p. 408.

36 Eliot quotations from T. S. Eliot, *Dante* (London: Faber and Faber, 1945), p. 46. Pearl on Dante, "half of the world," in *The Dante Club* (New York: Random House, 2002), p. viii. Pound on Dante's aristocracy in *The Poet's Dante* (New York: FSG, 2000), p. 9.

37 Love as unhappiness, in Eco, *Travels in Hyperreality,* p. 64

37 *"is the soul seen by itself."* Quoted in Giuseppe Mazzotta, *Dante's Vision and the Circle of Knowledge* (Princeton: Princeton University Press), p. 136.

Chapter Three

42 Inferno's *first two cantos:* The dates of the first two cantos are highly debated among Dante scholars.

43 The largeness of Boniface's aims, in Lonsdale Ragg, *Dante and His Italy* (London: Methuen, 1907), p. 27.

44 Celestine history, in Durant, p. 812.

46 *Unam Sanctum,* in Henry Osborn Taylor, *The Medieaval Mind: A History of the Development of Thought and Emotion in the Middle Ages* (Cambridge: Harvard University Press, 1971), p. 539.

46 *"exactly as the Senators":* Ragg, p. 37.

48 *Boniface is not dead:* Ragg, p. 39.

49 *The end of Boniface:* Jules Michelet, *History of France: From the Earliest Period to the Present Day* (New York: Appleton, 1845).

50 Saint Francis material, in G. K. Chesterton, *Saint Francis of Assisi* (New York: Image Books, Doubleday, 1990).

52 *"If life is art":* Chesterton, p. 65.

54 bread turns bile into blood: in Caroline Waller Bynum, *The Resurrection of the Body in Western Christianity, 200–1336* (New York: Columbia University Press, 1995).

54 *"Whenever poverty is not observed":* Charles T. Davis, *Dante's Italy* (Philadelphia: University of Pennsylvania Press, 1984).

55 Giotto's windfall, in Durant, pp. 609–13.

56 *The saint chased after poverty:* Chesterton, p. 81.

56 *changing worthless goods:* Michelet, p. 365.

57 *The way to build a church:* Chesterton, p. 57.

58 *The new crusader:* Michelet, pp. 364–66.

59 Observations and comments on Eliot, in Lyndall Gordon, *T. S. Eliot: An Imperfect Life* (New York: Norton, 1999)—"prophetic power," p. 74; sublime knowledge, p. 75.

61 Eliot comments, in Gordon, pp. 113, 147, 149, 152.

62 Keats biography, in Stephen Coote, *John Keats: A Life* (London: Hodder & Stoughton, 1996).

Chapter Four

66 *Bononia Docet:* in Arthur Symons, *Cities of Italy* (New York: Dutton, 1907), p. 243.

67 *appeal to the mind:* Kantorowicz, pp. 337–38.

68 *Peter of Abano:* Durant, p. 956.

68 Biographical evidence of Guido Cavalcanti, in Maria Luisa Ardizzone, *Guido Cavalcanti: The Other Middle Ages* (Toronto: University of Toronto Press, 2002), pp. 37–40.

69 *"Where is the border":* Pound in David Anderson, *Pound's Cavalcanti: An Edition of the Translations, Notes and Essays* (Princeton: Princeton University Press, 1983), p. 209.

71 *Today, where are the students:* René Guénon, *Fundamental Symbols: The Universal Language of Sacred Science,* comp. and ed. Michel Valson, trans. Alvin Moore, Jr. (Cambridge: Quinta Essentia, 1995).

76 Chapters xix–xxxi of *Vita Nuova* replace Guido Cavalcanti's influences with that of the "other Guido"—Guinizelli.

77 *Dante's Hell will have:* John Freccero class notes, NYU, Fall 2001.

77 *Bolognese students rush around, etc.*: Symons, p. 239.

78 *connected by their conflict and their fanaticism, by a spiritual and poetic field*: Denis de Rougement, *Love in the Western World*, trans. Montgomery Belgion (New York: Schocken, 1983), p. 361.

78 Comparison to Hegel master / slave parable, in Freccero notes.

78 *Death, such as it is, comes from mortification*: Robert C. Solo-mon, *In the Spirit of Hegel: A Study of G. W. F. Hegel's Phenomenonology of Spirit* (New York: Oxford University Press, 1983), p. 446.

79 *The fifth meeting place of the Templars*: Eco, *Foucault's Pendulum*, p. 123, and Partner on Templar history and Dante, p. 56.

80 *"We wanted mercy and you gave us knowledge"*: in John Guare, *Love's Fire: Seven Plays Inspired by Shakespearean Sonnets* (New York: Quill, 1998).

84 Biographical data on Lorenzo, in Judith Hook, *Lorenzo de' Medici: An Historical Biography* (London: Hamish Hamilton, 1984).

Chapter Five

87 *The Thomist method*: Frances Yates, *The Art of Memory* (Chicago: University of Chicago Press, 1974), p. 101.

88 *"The terrifying gargoyles"*: Yates, p. 104.

88 *Everything from Gothic cathedrals*: Émile Mâle, *Religious Art from the Twelfth to the Eighteenth Century* (New York: Noonday Press, 1963), p. ix.

90 *"With St. Thomas"*: Émile Mâle, *Gothic Image: Religious Art in France of the Thirteenth Century*, trans. Dora Nussey (New York: Harper, 1958), p. 13.

90 *"The most ardent imagination"*: Mâle, *Gothic Image*, p. 13.

94 Freccero compares the *Comedy* to a Mobius strip, in his class lectures.

95 *To come close to the human-divine boundary* and *God's habit of working:* Jesse M. Gellrich, *The Idea of the Book in the Middle Ages: Language Theory, Mythology and Fiction* (Ithaca and London: Cornell University Press, 1985), pp. 139–66.

95 *"a place for everything":* C. S. Lewis, *The Discarded Image* (London: Cambridge University Press, 1964), pp. 10–11.

96 Simonides, in Yates, pp. 1–2.

98 *lines are the substance:* Osip Mandelstam, *Selected Essays,* ed. Sidney Monas (Austin and London: University of Texas Press, 1977), p. 39.

100 Details on the first manuscripts of the *Comedy,* the dying and deformed Gothic script and *bastarde,* in Armando Petrucci, *Writers and Readers in Medieval Italy: Studies in the History of Written Culture* (New Haven: Yale University Press, 1995), pp. 198–99.

100 *To put "pen to paper":* Christopher de Hamel, *Medieval Craftsmen: Scribes and Illuminators* (London: British Museum Press, 1992), p. 28.

100 *The world is itself a book:* Gellrich, pp. 29–50.

101 *Increasingly, however, works like the Comedy:* Petrucci, pp. 173–74.

101 *Dante is a copyist:* Mandelstam, p. 39.

101 *An Irish codex of the twelfth century:* Illich, p. 109.

101 *"I will labor a little more":* Mandelstam, p. 39.

102 Perfumers/destroyers, in Marc Drogin, *Anathema! Medieval*

Scribes and the History of Book Curses (Montclair, N.J.: Allanheld & Schram, 1983).

104 *"poetic ethics"*: Marianne Shapiro, *De Vulgari Eloquentia: Dante's Book of Exile* (Lincoln and London: University of Nebraska Press, 1990), p. 41.

106 *Ten years after Dante's death:* Roger Chartier, "The Practical Impact of Writing," in David Finkelstein and Alistair McCleery, eds., *The Book History Reader* (London and New York: Routledge, 2002), p. 123.

107 *"the panther whose fragrance":* Shapiro, p. 28.

107 Ancient history of the panther, in Marcel Detienne, *Dionysos Slain* (Baltimore: Johns Hopkins Press, 1977), pp. 37–39.

107 Wicksteed quotation in Chubb, *Dante and His World,* p. 541.

108 The Dante panther in Umberto Eco, *The Search for the Perfect Language* (London: Blackwell Publishers, Ltd., 1995), p. 45.

108 *Dantean Pilgrimages:* Mark A. Peterson, "Galileo's Discovery of Scaling Laws," *American Journal of Physics* 70, no. 6 (June 2002), pp. 575–80.

109 Peter Pesic, "Comment on 'Galileo's Discovery of Scaling Laws,' by Mark A. Peterson," *American Journal of Physics* 70, no. 11 (November 2002), pp. 1160–61.

Chapter Six

111 Levi's experience, in Primo Levi, "The Canto of Ulysses," in *Survival in Auschwitz: The Nazi Assault on Humanity,* trans. Stuart Woolf (New York: Collier/Macmillan, 1993), pp. 109–15; and Risa B. Soldi, *A Dante of Our Time: Primo Levi and Auschwitz* (New York: Peter Lang, 1990), pp. 68–71.

114 Gemini characteristics, in Isabelle Pagan, *From Pioneer to Poet: The Twelve Great Gates* (London: Theosophical Publishing House, 1969), p. 43.

117 *The problem is the "sea of existence":* Hans Blumenberg, *Shipwreck with Spectator: Paradigm of a Metaphor for Existence,* trans. Steven Rendall (Cambridge and London: Cambridge University Press, 1997), p. 20ff.

117 Eliot was also inspired in "Animula" by *Purgatorio* 26, lines 85–93.

118 Hadrian's "Animula" may also be translated to indicate that it is not the soul that is stiff but "the pallid places, stark and bare," to which the soul goes, in Marguerite Yourcenar's version.

119 *another heroic enterprise:* John Freccero, *Dante: The Poetics of Conversion,* ed. Rachel Jacoff (Cambridge, Mass.: Harvard University Press, 1986), pp. 112–20, 144.

121 *His deception ended up:* Giuseppe Mazzotta, "Canto 26," in Mandelbaum et al., *Lectura Dantis: Inferno,* p. 355.

121 *He believed in promises:* Mazzotta, *Dante's Vision,* p. 67.

121 Shelley biography, in Richard Holmes, *Shelley: The Pursuit* (London: Flamingo, 1995), pp. 727ff.

122 *"Speech," says a sarcastic divine:* John S. Carroll, *Prisoners of Hope: An Exposition of Dante's Purgatorio* (Port Washington, N.Y.: Kennikat Press, 1971).

122 Latini quotations, in Giuseppe Mazzotta, *Dante, Poet of the Desert: History and Allegory in the* Divine Comedy (Princeton: Princeton University Press, 1979), pp. 18–21.

123 *"salesmen of words":* Augustine, *Confessions* I. 13.

124 *He is afraid of possible treachery:* Mazzotta, *Dante, Poet of the Desert,* p. 105.

125 *Rhetoric is a tool to manipulate:* Mazotta, *Dante, Poet of the Desert,* p. 72ff.

126 *"to teach you how to make better prayers":* Robert Hollander, *Dante Studies,* CXI (1993), p. 21.

126 *For him, the journey is the poem:* Freccero, *Dante,* p. 146.

128 *Here penitents are nourished:* William Warren Vernon, *Readings on the Purgatorio of Dante, Chiefly Based on the Commentary of Benvenuto da Imola,* vol. II (London: Methuen, 1907), p. 369.

131 Machiavelli and astuteness, in Sebastian de Grazia, *Machiavelli in Hell* (Princeton: Princeton University Press, 1989), p. 203.

Chapter Seven

136 The Zohar's travels, in Gershom Scholem, *Major Trends in Jewish Mysticism* (New York: Schocken, 1974), p. 156ff.

137 Ecstasy, zeal, liquefaction, etc., in Dante Alighieri, *Inferno,* trans. Allen Mandelbaum (New York: Bantam, 1982), p. xvi.

138 Dante and Exodus is an argument developed by Freccero in *Dante,* pp. 58–69.

139 *Emperors had for centuries:* Hollander, *Dante: A Life in Works,* p. 4.

140 *He will need to curb art:* Dante Alighieri, *Purgatorio,* trans. Allen Mandelbaum (New York: Bantam Books, 1984), p. xviii.

141 Bernard of Clairvaux history, in James Cotter Morison, *The Life and Times of Saint Bernard, Abbot of Clairvaux* (London: Macmillan,

1868), and G. R. Evans, *Bernard of Clairvaux* (New York: Oxford University Press, 2000).

142 *two of the gifts of the Magi:* Robert Graves, *The White Goddess: A Historical Grammar of Poetic Myth* (New York: Noonday, 1966), p. 396.

142 *She transformed Catholicism:* Durant, p. 747.

143 Adams on the Virgin Mary: in Henry Adams, *Mont Saint Michel and Chartres* (New York: Penguin, 1986), pp. 87–102.

144 History of Purgatory, in Jacques Le Goff, *The Birth of Purgatory,* trans. Arthur Goldhammer (Chicago: University of Chicago Press, 1984); and mathematical concept of intermediacy, in Le Goff, p. 7.

146 *lettuce being eaten by a nun:* Durant, p. 734.

146 *Mary became the star:* Jaroslav Pelikan, *Mary Through the Centuries: Her Place in the History of Culture* (New Haven: Yale University Press, 1996), pp. 93–94.

148 Ancient views on art, in Frederick Artz, *The Mind of the Middle Ages: An Historical Survey, A.D. 200–1500* (Chicago: University of Chicago Press, 1980), pp. 384–403.

148 *For Dante, it was to find:* Bynum, pp. 87–88.

149 Notion of *Penelopiad* from Lowenstam, conversation.

149 Clare of Montefalco in E. A. Foran, *Life of St. Clare of the Cross* (London: Burns, Oates & Washbourne, Ltd., 1935), pp. 71–76. Delivering the *Inferno* to Ilario, in Chubbs, pp. 548–49.

152 Argument on women's prime role in *Purgatorio,* in Joan Ferrante, *Woman as Image in Medieval Literature: From the Twelfth Century to Dante* (New York and London: Columbia University Press, 1975), p. 129ff.

152 Beauty's minimal relationship to art, in Katharine Everett Gilbert and Helmut Kuhn, *A History of Aesthetics* (New York: Macmillan, 1939).

153 Notion of decentering and unselfing, in Elaine Scarry, *On Beauty and Being Just* (Princeton: Princeton University Press, 1999), p. 57–124.

154 *"Mystification" was a good word:* Freccero class notes.

154 *"To Dante, the good and great":* Yates, p. 54.

155 *She is the continuing source:* Joan M. Ferrante, *Dante's Beatrice: Priest of an Androgynous God* (Binghamton, New York: Center for Medieval and Early Renaissance Studies, 1992), pp. 1–2 and ff.

156 Fellini filmography, in Donald P. Costello, *Fellini's Road* (Notre Dame and London: University of Notre Dame Press, 1983.

Chapter Eight

157 Beckett quotation, in Anthony Cronin, *Samuel Beckett: The Last Modernist* (New York: Da Capo, 1999), p. 568.

157 Eliot, p. 45.

157 Longfellow, in *The Divine Comedy of Dante Alighieri*, trans. Henry Wadsworth Longfellow (Boston: Houghton Mifflin, 1895), p. 611.

159 *Dante left the ant heap of turmoil:* John White, *Art and Architecture in Italy, 1250 to 1400* (New York: Penguin, 1987), p. 452.

160 *"Greatest works":* John H. Finley, *Homer's Odyssey* (Cambridge, Mass: Harvard University Press, 1978), p. 171.

162 *Beginning in the early fourteenth century:* Joseph R. Strayer, ed., *Dictionary of the Middle Ages* (New York: Scribner, 1987), vol. 9, p. 405.

163 *For Hugh, knowledge was not light:* Illich, p. 15ff.

163 *Bacon was thrown into prison:* Jean Gimpel, *The Cathedral Builders* (New York: Grove, 1980), p. 119.

164 *Given that most people:* Michael Camille, *Gothic Art: Glorious Visions* (New York: Prentice Hall and Harry N. Abrams, 1996), p. 29.

165 Hans Jantzen, *High Gothic: The Classic Cathedrals of Chartres, Reims, Amiens* (Princeton: Princeton University Press, 1984), p. 69.

165 *the twelfth-century glassworker:* Adams, p. 126.

166 *"weak little frame":* Erwin Panofsky, *Abbot Suger on the Abbey Church of St.-Denis and Its Art Treasures* (Princeton: Princeton University Press, 1979), p. 32.

166 *As a "beggar lifted up":* Panofsky, p. 33.

166 *on one side the suffering Savior:* Robert W. Hanning, "Suger's Literary Style and Vision," in Paula Lieber Gerson, ed., *Abbot Suger and Saint-Denis* (New York: Metropolitan Museum of Art, 1986), p. 146.

166 *Or did he love beauty:* Umberto Eco, *The Aesthetics of Thomas Aquinas,* trans. Hugh Bredin (Cambridge, Mass: Harvard University Press, 1988), p. 14.

166 *"a workshop of Vulcan":* in Danielle Gaborit-Chopin, "Suger's Liturgical Vessels," in Gerson, p. 292.

167 *When some exceptionally long beams:* Panofsky, p. 34.

168 *stunningly simple dramas of forked lightning:* John Ruskin, "On the Nature of the Gothic," in *The Stones of Venice* (New York and London: Penguin, 2001), p. 177.

168 *Even the Ravenna mosaics:* Adams, p. 124.

169 *Suger's methods of building:* Camille, p. 37.

170 *The "secret" by which Suger:* pp. 57–58 in Paul Frankl, "The Secret of the Medieval Masons," *Art Bulletin,* March 1945, pp. 46–60.

171 *"the element of Cistercian austerity":* Otto von Simson, *The Gothic Cathedral: Origins of Gothic Architecture and the Medieval Concept of Order* (New York: Harper Torchbook, 1964), p. 112.

171 Details of medieval Paris, in Christopher Hare, *Dante the Way-farer* (London: Harper & Brothers, 1905); and Mildred Prica Bjerken, *Medieval Paris: The Town of Books* (Metuchen, N.J.: Scarecrow Press, 1973).

172 *There were three kinds of light:* Eco, *Art and Beauty in the Middle Ages,* trans. Hugh Bredin (New Haven: Yale University Press, 1986), p. 50.

172 Boethius history, in Howard Rollin Patch, *The Tradition of Boethius: A Study of His Importance in Medieval Culture* (New York: Oxford University Press, 1935).

174 *Anything beautiful involves the invisible:* Urban Tigner Holmes, Jr., *Daily Living in the Twelfth Century* (Madison: University of Wisconsin Press, 1952), p. 237ff.

174 *Evil itself became good:* Mazzotta, *Dante's Vision,* p. 35. Discussion of geometry and medieval vision in chapter 10, page 197ff.

175 *Commedia* math, in Vincent Foster Hopper, *Medieval Number Symbolism* (New York: Cooper Square, 1969), pp. 136–201.

176 *"Unity is the beginning of number":* Charles S. Singleton, *Paradiso 2: Commentary* (Princeton: Bollingen Paperback, Princeton University Press, 1977), p. 255.

176 *One might see Dante's consummate challenge:* Freccero class notes.

179 *God can be described:* Freccero class notes.

180 Schlegel quote: Nicholas Maiston, *Schumann: Fantasie, Op. 17* (Cambridge: Cambridge University Press, 1992), p. 1. The pianist referred to here is internationally renowned Jeffrey Kahare.

180 *"When you finally manage":* Freccero class notes.

181 *The news must have reached him in Paris:* Chubb, p. 614.

182 *Giuseppe Terragni:* Thomas L. Schumacher, *The Danteum: A Study in the Architecture of Literature* (Princeton, N.J: Princeton Architectural Press, 1985), pp. 18–20.

Chapter Nine

183 Arno valley dominated by castles, in Chubb, p. 259.

184 *He has given up fighting:* Etienne Gilson, *Dante the Philosopher,* trans. David Moore (New York: Sheed & Ward, 1949), p. 172.

185 *Dante will have to confront everything:* Peter Hawkins, *Dante's Testaments: Essays in Scriptural Imagination* (Stanford: Stanford University Press, 1999), p. 7.

187 *butterfly image:* Freccero class notes.

188 Beethoven's hearing loss, in Maynard Solomon, *Beethoven* (New York: Schirmer, 1998), p. 158.

188 Why Beethoven accepts his loss, in Solomon, p. 161.

188 *"For a poet to lose":* Clive James, *As of This Writing: The Essential Essays 1968–2002* (New York: Norton, 2003), p. 14.

190 Louse eggs quotation, in Chubb, p. 631.

190 Clement offering Henry a dull weapon, in Chubb, pp. 604–11.

191 Tuscany shaped like a heart, in Root, *The Food of Italy,* p. 28.

191 Stories about Virgil, in John Webster Spargo, *Virgil the Necromancer: Studies in Virgilian Legends* (Cambridge, Mass.: Harvard University Press, 1934).

193 Arnaut Daniel biography and poetry in James J. Wilhelm, ed. and trans., *The Poetry of Arnaut Daniel* (New York: Garland, 1981), p. xix.

195 *"Dante's is the parable":* Leo Spitzer, *Linguistics and Literary History: Essays in Stylistics* (Princeton: Princeton University Press, 1948), p. 169.

201 *Virgil's fear* and *the work of generations:* Geoffrey L. Bickersteth, *Dante's Virgil: A Poet's Poet* (Glasgow: Jackson, Son & Co. [Glasgow University Publications, LXXXIX], 1951).

204 *Brunetto "falls so far behind":* John Freccero in Rachel Jacoff and Jeffrey Schnap, eds., *The Poetry of Allusion: Virgil and Ovid in Dante's Commedia* (Stanford: Stanford University Press, 1991), p. 71.

Chapter Ten

209 Dante's hates, in Durant, p. 1080.

209 *"opposite Eden":* in Charles S. Singleton, *Journey to Beatrice* (Baltimore: Johns Hopkins University Press, 1977).

210 *"Dante's ass,"* Catherine Mary Phillimore, *Dante at Ravenna: A Study* (London: E. Stock, 1898), p. 142.

212 The Scaligers' ambitions, in John Julius Norwich, *A History of Venice* (New York: Vintage, 1989), p. 205.

212 *He is said never to be afraid:* H. V. Morton, *A Traveller in Italy* (London: Methuen, 1984), p. 299.

212 Anecdote about Cangrande's brother, in Chubb, p. 499.

212 *"If the halls of the Hermitage":* Mandelstam, *Collected Essays*, p. 440.

214 The Roman Empire dying at Ravenna, in Morton, p. 259.

215 *"Three times Western civilization":* Otto G. von Simson, *Sacred Fortress: Byzantine Art and Statecraft in Ravenna* (Princeton: Princeton University Press, 1987), p. 1.

215 *devious lagoons:* in Durant, p. 28.

215 enemies from the different camps: in Simson, pp. 1–18.

216 How Christ won the world, and the House of Bread, in H. E. Jacob, *Six Thousand Years of Bread* (Garden City, N.Y.: Doubleday, 1944), pp. 107–8.

217 *In the churches, the mosaics:* André Grabar, *Byzantine Painting* (Paris: Éditions d' Art Albert Skira, World Publishing Co., 1953), p. 68.

218 *The answer in Paradise:* Jeffrey Burton Russell, *A History of Heaven: The Singing Silence* (Princeton: Princeton University Press, 1997), p. 186.

218 Commentary on *Paradiso* drawn from Russell.

219 *The passion of earthly love:* Russell, p. 173.

219 *His long absorption:* Dante Alighieri, *The Paradiso,* trans. John Ciardi (New York: Signet Classic, 2001), p. 177ff.

221 *"If a spoon":* Russell, p. 179.

223 *If we are looking for a point:* Freccero, *Dante,* p. 90.

224 Image of *Paradiso*'s likeness in the surface of a glass building, in Freccero class notes.

224 *Dante's "amorosa lima":* Ezra Pound, "From *Dante,*" in *A Poet's Dante,* p. 10.

226 *Physics cannot hope for reliability:* Alison Cornish, *Reading Dante's Stars* (New Haven: Yale University Press, 2000), p. 9.

227 *Pietro, a successful lawyer:* Phillimore, p. 130ff.

227 Ravenna versus Venico: Chubb, p. 788ff.

227 *"not of the sun":* Hugh Kenner, *The Pound Era* (Berkeley: University of California Press, 1971), p. 348.

228 *He made his way back:* Norwich, p. 204.

228 Boccaccio's story in Giovanni Boccaccio, *The Life of Dante,* in *The Earlier Lives of Dante,* trans. J. R. Smith (New York: Holt, 1901), p. 65.

230 Report of Dante's open grave, in Phillimore, p. 198ff.

231 *Dante's whole journey in Paradise:* Freccero class notes.

232 *The love of truth* and the story of Aquinas's dying, in G. K. Chesterton, *Saint Thomas Aquinas: "The Dumb Ox"* (New York: Image Books/Doubleday, 1956), p. 138.

234   Distrust of bakers and millers, in Jacob, p. 140.

234   *Dantean Journey:* Barbara Reynolds, *The Passionate Intellect: Dorothy L. Sayers' Encounter with Dante* (Kent, Ohio: Kent State University Press, 1989), pp. 191–206.

236   "Plaque or wall: Symons, *Cities of Italy,* p. 185.

Acknowledgments

I OWE MY greatest thanks to Alice Mayhew, legendary editor. She is proof that the blue pencil is mightier than the keyboard. She is a teacher, collaborator, inspirer, and is unsentimental in carrying out all these roles. I could say much more, but I imagine her drawing a line through all the adjectives I can conjure.

Glen Hartley and Lyn Chiu, my agents, have been unflagging in encouragement and support.

A very special thanks to John Freccero, the grand master of Danteana. Freccero makes criticism poetry. I believe he knows more about Dante than Dante knew about himself. Another superlative teacher, John Hollander, is known for generosity and perspicacity. Through his books and e-mail, he made both available to me. Simone Marchesi of Princeton University read the manuscript; my gratitude for his corrections.

Naming these scholars impels me to warn the reader of the gulf between their work and mine. This is not a work of scholarship. I am an impressionable reader who imagines her life begins with Dante and who has tracked her hero into the High Middle Ages. The records are sparse; the sources often contradict one another on such basic elements as the number of Dante's children. I have relied on sources considered most credible, but even then the reader should bear in mind that medieval accuracy resides in the shadows of history.

So many souls I met on this journey made life grand: the brilliant and spirited David Rosenthal, publisher of Simon & Schuster, and Associate Editor Emily Takoudes, a gifted young editor who is also balletic in her execution of the most onerous tasks. Thanks also to the University of Oregon's Knight Library, one of the great libraries in the West. Thanks too to Sally Johnson of the General Theological Seminary in New York, and to the extraordinary staff at the American Academy in Rome, managed by Pina Pasquantonio and led by AAR's incomparable director, Adele Chatfield-Taylor. Dina Dineva created the beautiful index, a poem in itself.

Janet Corcoran and Susan Clampitt: thanks for your unstinting generosity: you both deserve a petal of your own in the Rose of Paradise. Conversations with Nathan Schwartz-Salant, Betty Sue Flowers and Larry Allums made it possible to go from page to page of this manuscript daunted but undeterred.

And special thanks to Steven Lowenstam, Stefano, teacher and guide, classicist and husband: the diagnosis of his brain tumor plunged us into Infernal and Purgatorial worlds; his love and courage were Paradisal. He read this book chapter by chapter as it was written. His comments and our conversations were chief among the joys of my life. For leading me to all these people, I thank the guide of guides, Dante.

Index

Index

About the Author

Harriet Rubin was the founder of Doubleday Currency and published dozens of bestsellers. She has been a columnist and writer for *Fast Company* and is on *USA TODAY*'s editorial board, as well as being a consultant to media companies. Her book *The Princessa: Machiavelli for Women* was translated into twenty-three languages. She currently lives in Manhattan and Eugene, Oregon.